shortcuts to success

indian

Das Sreedharan

photography by Peter Cassidy

First published in the UK in 2003 by Quadrille Publishing Limited
Alhambra House, 27-31 Charing Cross Road, London WC2H OLS

This edition published by Silverback Books, Inc., San Francisco, California. www.silverbackbooks.com
© in 2005

Editorial director Jane O'Shea Creative director Helen Lewis
Managing editor Janet Illsley Art director Vanessa Courtier Editor Jenni Muir
Photographer Peter Cassidy Food stylist Sunil Vijayakar Props stylist Jane Campsie
Copy editor Kathy Steer Designer Sue Storey Production Beverley Richardson and Vincent Smith

Text © 2003 Das Sreedharan Photography © 2003 Pete Cassidy
Design and layout © 2003 Quadrille Publishing Limited

Cataloguing in Publication Data: a catalogue record for this book is available from the British Library.

ISBN 1 59637 012 2
Printed in China

contents

NOTES

Measurements are in standard American cups and spoons.

Use fresh herbs unless dried herbs are suggested.

Use freshly ground black pepper unless otherwise stated.

Eggs from cage-free or free-range hens are recommended, and extra large eggs should be used except where a different size is specified.

Recipes that feature raw or lightly cooked eggs should be avoided by vulnerable people (anyone who is pregnant, babies and young children, the elderly, and those who are sick or who have compromised immune systems), unless using eggs pasteurized in shell.

introduction

Although people everywhere love to eat Indian food, many have put off cooking it at home because they believe the dishes are too complicated and require a lot of strange ingredients. To me, this is a sad misperception. Throughout India, there are many wonderful examples of simple home cooking using ingredients readily available on supermarket shelves all over the world. There is nothing I would like better than to tell you more about these recipes.

Since moving to England and establishing my first restaurant, it has been my mission to promote the kind of food I was fortunate enough to enjoy while growing up in Kerala, South India's largest state. Like most people, I still think my mother is the best cook in the world! Many of the dishes I prepare today—whether in the restaurants, during my cooking evenings for customers, or at home with my wife, Alison—are those I adored when I was young. Like many Indians, our family was vegetarian and daily meals were healthy combinations of fresh vegetables, fruits, yogurt, and nuts, with many of the ingredients grown in our own garden.

Over the years I have also collected many recipes from friends and colleagues while traveling throughout India. The ones I have chosen for this book come from various communities with substantially different religious and cultural traditions. Like the South Indian recipes (which are themselves from a lively cultural mix), they use ingredients that are easy to find and methods that are simple and quick. There are meat dishes, including Goan pork vindaloo and Kashmiri lamb rojan josh, chicken and vegetable dishes from Bengal, and many recipes using the dairy products and legumes beloved throughout North India.

In addition, I am including several of our restaurants' most popular dishes and new creations developed during my cooking evenings. I really enjoy taking ingredients such as zucchini and cauliflower, which I never knew as a child, and creating new Indian dishes from them. Fusing Northern and Southern Indian cooking styles is also a great passion, but that doesn't mean the resulting dishes are complicated—some of them contain as few as six ingredients.

A few Indian techniques, such as making spice blends, may seem a little daunting at first, but you will be astonished at how quick and easy they are. The blender you already use to blend soups until smooth works equally well as a grinder for producing fragrant pastes, sauces, and batters. Soon you will be doing so with confidence, as well as quickly grating fresh coconut in the food processor, and softening tamarind pulp to add a sour, fruity flavor to curries.

My mother always said that no one can teach you to cook. She said: "I will show you how I do it, but you have to learn to do it your way." This is an important tradition in India. You should feel free to adapt the quantities of spices, oil, water, and main ingredients given in these recipes to suit your own taste. I do hope that you enjoy using this book and that it inspires you to cook more often. It doesn't matter whether the food you prepare is South Indian, North Indian, or Italian. I honestly believe that home cooking is the foundation of good health and happiness.

ingredients

You won't need an extensive array of spices and authentic flavorings to prepare my recipes, but here is a guide to the special ingredients that are featured in this book.

Banana leaves

Banana leaves are used in South India, as well as in Central and South America, the Caribbean, and Southeast Asia, to wrap foods for cooking (such as fish for steaming), in much the same way as aluminum foil is used in North America and Europe. They can also take the place of serving plates.

You can find fresh banana leaves in Asian and Latin markets. To use the leaves in cooking, first soften by holding over a flame or dipping in a dish of warm water for 30 seconds. This will make the leaves pliable and easy to fold.

Chana dal

These robust yellow legumes are a brown variety of pea that is skinned and split. They look very similar to yellow split peas and have a sweet and nutty aroma. Chana dal is combined with meat in curries, ground with lamb to make a paste for kebabs, and frequently cooked with vegetables, especially squashes. In Kerala, it is used to make sweet as well as savory dishes.

Chili peppers

The wide range of chili peppers available today can be confusing, but in Keralan dishes and for the recipes featured in this book, there are only two types that you need: small, dried, very hot, red chili peppers, about 1–1½ inches long, and fresh, medium-hot, green chili peppers about 3 inches long.

Chili peppers are renowned for being fiery hot, and this makes some people wary of them. However, their heat can be controlled. You can bring chili flavor to a recipe without strong heat by using the chili whole rather than slicing or chopping it. To do this, cut a slit about two-thirds of the way along the length of the chili before adding it to the pan. Another way of reducing chili heat is by removing the seeds before slicing or chopping chili peppers.

Coconut

The large, hairy, brown coconut is indigenous to several areas, one of which is South India, and the freshly grated white meat of the nut is essential to Keralan cooking. It is used in an amazing variety of ways, including vegetable side dishes, breads, curries, savory snacks, and sweet dishes, and appears in some form at every meal.

Unsweetened dried shredded coconut can often be used in place of freshly grated coconut in dishes, but as it has a much drier texture the result is not as succulent. It is far better to use the fresh nut.

To extract the meat from a fresh coconut, insert a metal skewer in the "eye" of the coconut and drain the water into a jug. Using a heavy tool, such as a cleaver, carefully crack the shell around the middle, then separate the inner nut from the hairy casing. You can then use a vegetable peeler to make long shavings of coconut meat, or an ordinary kitchen grater to grate it. When only a small amount is required, a citrus zester will give you fine shreds quickly and easily. To prepare a substantial quantity of fresh coconut, place the pieces of coconut meat in a food processor and process until minced.

Coconut milk

Do not confuse this with the clear water inside a fresh coconut. Coconut milk is a manufactured product, made by pouring hot water over grated coconut meat, then pressing in a strainer to give a thin, white liquid. Coconut cream is similar, but has a much thicker consistency. Coconut milk is used as the base for many South Indian dishes and is readily available in cans and long-life packs.

Curry leaves

Curry leaves, which come from a plant with the botanical name of *Murraya koenigi*, are thought to smell and taste like curry powder. While the taste is spicy, it is also nutty, a quality brought out when the curry leaves are lightly fried in oil until just crisp. They are used as herbs in cooking, most often added whole, but sometimes chopped first. Bay leaves may look similar, but they have a very different flavor and are not an appropriate substitute. Don't hesitate to buy a substantial bunch of curry leaves when you see them. For convenience, they can be stored in the freezer, wrapped in foil or sealed in a plastic bag, then added to dishes as and when required.

Ghee

Highly popular in North India, ghee is the Indian version of clarified butter—that is, butter which has had all its milk solids removed. The process involves melting the butter over a low heat, then simmering it until all the moisture has evaporated and the milk solids have separated from the fat. The milk solids are then removed to leave a pure fat that is excellent for frying at high temperatures. Ghee also has a long shelf life—so much so that it is sold in cans on the supermarket shelf rather than in the fresh dairy section.

Jaggery and palm sugar

An unrefined form of sugar, jaggery is dark, sticky, and crumbly. Made from the juice of crushed sugar cane, it is less sweet than ordinary white or brown sugars and has an extraordinary musky flavor. Palm sugar, from countries such as Thailand, has a comparable rich, complex taste and is a reasonable substitute for Indian jaggery in cooking. Brown sugar and "raw" sugars such as Turbinado and Demerara lack this earthy quality, but the recipes in this book will work if you use them instead.

Paneer

India's best-known cheese is often described as a "cottage" or "curd" cheese because it is usually freshly made in the home. However, paneer is drained and pressed, which makes it very different from cottage cheese. Paneer's firmer texture means it can be cut into cubes, then fried or broiled until golden brown, while still retaining its square shape.

Plantains

Sometimes referred to as cooking bananas, plantains look rather like large bananas, but have a thicker green skin and starchier, less sweet flesh. This fruit plays an important role in South Indian cooking and several different varieties grow in Kerala alone. When green, or unripe, they are used as a vegetable in curries, and when ripe they are steamed and eaten for breakfast.

Rice

Fragrant basmati rice is often regarded as the supreme Indian rice variety, but we tend not to use it on a daily basis in India because it is expensive compared with other locally grown varieties. Also, basmati rice has a unique aroma, which can be lost when combined with many strongly flavored ingredients. The recipes in this book indicate when regular long-grain white rice is appropriate.

Rice flour

Fine, white, powdery rice flour is commonly used for batters and doughs in South India, and to make soft rice noodle cakes. It can also be used as a thickening agent, in the same way as cornstarch. Rice flour has a mild flavor that is delicately sweet, but not so much that it detracts from savory dishes.

Spices

My home state of Kerala is known as the "spice box" of India, but I have limited the range of spices in this book, so you won't have to buy more than you are comfortable with. Spices that feature most often in my cooking include whole brown mustard seeds, ground turmeric, cumin, coriander, and cinnamon. Using mustard seeds in the way I do doesn't impart a strong mustard flavor, but instead adds a slightly crunchy texture. Turmeric is India's most widely used spice and brings a mellow flavor and golden color to dishes. Cumin is one of the most versatile spices. It can take on different flavors depending on how it is treated—used whole, ground, toasted, fried, or raw. Garam masala, which means "hot spices," is a convenient ready-made mix of ground spices, and is aromatic rather than fiery. Almost every Indian kitchen has its favorite garam masala blend, but most contain black peppercorns, cardamom, cinnamon, cumin, cloves, and mace.

Tamarind pulp

This tart fruit is used in South Indian and Gujarati cooking as a souring agent, and it brings a tangy contrast to mild coconut sauces. It is also used for chutneys and drinks. Sold in dried blocks, before use tamarind pulp needs to be soaked in hot water for about 20 minutes to soften the fruit, then pushed through a strainer to remove any seeds and fibers. The resulting liquid is stirred into dishes. Although the process of making tamarind liquid is always the same, recipes can vary in the intensity of liquid required, so the ratio of tamarind to hot water varies accordingly.

Urad dal

The small black lentils used to make urad dal are found in a variety of forms in India. In the North, the whole black lentils are favored, while in Southern India (and in all of my recipes) the lentils are invariably skinned and split. Although these are also known as black gram dal, the term is confusing because South Indian urad dal is cream in color. Urad dal is rather like a spice, added to dishes to provide a nutty flavor and crunchy texture.

Yogurt

Thick and creamy yogurt is made every day in homes across the Indian subcontinent and is an important part of every meal, most commonly enjoyed plain as a mild contrast to spicy food. Raitas—cooling salads made with yogurt and crunchy vegetables—are very popular. Yogurt is also often churned into cooling drinks with spices, and is the base for many desserts. In savory cooking, its main role is as a souring agent. Any thick, creamy, plain yogurt will work for the recipes in this book, but avoid any brands that are very sharp and acidic in flavor.

1 appetizers, snacks, and chutneys

mushroom and coconut uthappams

These rice pancakes are South India's answer to pizza. You can use any seasonal crunchy vegetables and herbs for the topping and the result can be very colorful. Uthappams are traditionally eaten with coconut chutney (page 30) and sometimes an elaborate sour lentil dish called sambar, but as long as your toppings are interesting, they are perfectly delicious served alone. Fenugreek seeds enhance the batter, but they are pungent, so remember a little goes a very long way.

MAKES 8
1³/₄ cups long-grain rice
¹/₂ cup dried urad dal
¹/₂ teaspoon fenugreek seeds
vegetable oil for frying
sea salt

FOR THE TOPPING:
1¹/₄ cups sliced mushrooms
1 red onion, peeled and finely sliced or chopped
2 medium-hot green chili peppers
2 tablespoons chopped cilantro or
    curry leaves
¹/₃ cup freshly grated coconut

1 Place the rice in a large bowl and cover with cold water. Put the urad dal and fenugreek seeds in another bowl and add sufficient cold water to cover generously. Set both bowls aside and let soak for at least 8 hours or overnight.

2 Drain the rice and dal, keeping them separate. Put the rice in a blender and process slowly for 2–3 minutes, gradually adding ¹/₂ cup water to make a smooth paste. Transfer to a large bowl. Place the urad dal and fenugreek seeds in the rinsed-out blender and process slowly for 5 minutes, gradually adding ¹/₄ cup water to make a batter. Add the dal mixture to the rice paste and mix well. Stir in a little salt and cover with a damp cloth. Set aside to ferment for 12 hours or overnight.

3 When ready to cook, the batter should have increased in volume and become a mass of small bubbles. Stir a little water into the batter to give a thick, pourable consistency. Heat a griddle or large, heavy-based frying pan until very hot, then lightly brush with oil. Assemble the topping ingredients and divide into 8 portions.

4 Pour a ladleful of the batter onto the griddle and spread it out slightly with the back of a spoon until about 4 inches in diameter. Top with a portion of the mushrooms, onion, chili, and cilantro or curry leaves, pressing them gently into the batter, then sprinkle lightly with the coconut. Cook for 2 minutes or until the base is golden brown.

5 Brush the edges of the uthappam with oil and carefully turn it over with a spatula. Cook on the other side for 2–3 minutes until the batter is cooked and the onion and mushrooms have browned slightly. Remove and keep warm while you cook the remaining uthappams. Serve with coconut chutney (page 30) or as a bread-like accompaniment to "wet" curries.

lentil and spinach vadai

"Vadai! Vadai! Vadai!" is the typical hawker cry heard in most railway stations in India. These crunchy, coarsely ground lentil patties are also very popular afternoon snacks in teashops. They have an amazing flavor and can be made with various lentils, but this version featuring chana dal is one of my favorites. If you are unable to find chana dal, substitute yellow split peas.

SERVES 4

2¹/₂ cups dried chana dal, or yellow split peas

7 oz spinach leaves, tough stems removed

1 onion, peeled and minced

2 medium-hot green chili peppers, minced

1-inch piece fresh ginger, peeled and minced

10 curry leaves, minced

vegetable oil for deep-frying

sea salt

1 Place the chana dal in a large bowl, cover with water, and set aside to soak for 1 hour. Meanwhile, place the spinach in a large saucepan over a low heat with just the water clinging to the leaves after washing, and cook, stirring occasionally, for 1 minute or until just wilted. Set aside to cool, then mince. Tip the soaked dal into a strainer and drain thoroughly.

2 Transfer the dal to a blender and process for 2–3 minutes to a coarse paste—don't grind it too finely as you want some of the dal to remain whole to give the vadai a good texture. Tip into a large bowl and add the minced spinach, onion, chilies, ginger, curry leaves, and a little salt. Mix thoroughly to make a thick paste.

3 Divide the mixture into portions about the size of a golf ball, then roll each one between your palms and gently flatten into a small, round patty. The mixture will make about 20 patties.

4 Heat the oil in a deep-fat fryer, wok, or large, heavy-based saucepan to 350°–375°F, or until a cube of bread browns in 30 seconds. Deep-fry the patties in batches for 5 minutes or until deep golden. Remove with a slotted spoon and drain on paper towels. Serve hot or cold.

onion bhajis

This is the simplest and cheapest snack you can make—no wonder it features on every Indian restaurant menu. To be honest, I wasn't keen on onion bhajis when I lived in India, but I became interested in them when I moved to London, where Muslim friends would make them for the Ramadan fast. Bhajis can be made with various vegetables, including greens, so don't hesitate to experiment with the basic recipe.
Illustrated on previous page

SERVES 4
2 onions, peeled and finely sliced
1¹/₂ cups chick pea flour
¹/₂ cup minced cilantro
¹/₂-inch piece fresh ginger, peeled and
  minced
¹/₂ teaspoon hot chili powder
¹/₂ teaspoon ground turmeric
pinch of crushed coriander seeds
vegetable oil for deep-frying
sea salt

1 In a large bowl, mix together the onion slices, chick pea flour, cilantro, ginger, chili powder, turmeric, crushed coriander seeds, and a little salt. Gradually mix in 2 cups water to make a thick batter.

2 Heat the oil in a deep-fat fryer, wok, or large, heavy-based saucepan to 350°–375°F, or until a cube of bread browns in 30 seconds. Using a metal spoon, take a small portion of batter and shape roughly into a ball, then carefully drop into the hot oil. Deep-fry for 3–4 minutes or until the bhaji is cooked through and has a crunchy, golden exterior. Cook the bhajis in batches of two or three, adding them to the oil one at a time. Remove with a slotted spoon and drain on paper towels. Serve hot.

bonda

The restaurants of Udupi in Karnataka are renowned for their bonda. These are incredibly tasty, filling snacks made with potatoes and subtly flavored with fresh ginger, curry leaves, and sometimes cashew nuts. Here, bonda are made special and more substantial by adding flavorsome ingredients such as chilies, onions, and cilantro. Tiny versions make great cocktail snacks. Serve with coconut chutney (page 30), sweet mango chutney (page 31), or with garlic and chili pickle (page 27).

SERVES 4

3 cups peeled and cubed potatoes
4 tablespoons vegetable oil
1 teaspoon mustard seeds
1 teaspoon dried urad dal
20 curry leaves
1-inch piece fresh ginger, peeled and
 grated
2 onions, peeled and minced
2 medium-hot green chili peppers, finely sliced
1 teaspoon ground turmeric, plus extra for
 seasoning
1/4 cup minced cilantro
1 cup chick pea flour
vegetable oil for deep-frying
sea salt

1 Cook the potatoes in a saucepan of lightly salted water for about 15 minutes until tender, then drain and mash. Set aside.

2 Heat the 4 tablespoons oil in a large frying pan. Add the mustard seeds and urad dal, and cook, stirring constantly, for 1–2 minutes or until the dal turns brown. Add the curry leaves, ginger, and onions, and cook, stirring occasionally, for 5 minutes.

3 Add the chilies and turmeric, and cook for 1 more minute before adding the mashed potatoes and cilantro. Stir over a low heat for 1 minute to ensure that the ingredients are thoroughly mixed, then remove the frying pan from the heat and set aside to cool.

4 Place the chick pea flour, a pinch of turmeric, and a pinch of salt in a large bowl, then gradually stir in 1 cup + 1 tablespoon water to make a smooth batter. Whisk until thoroughly blended, then set aside for 5 minutes.

5 Divide the potato mixture into small balls about the size of a golf ball. Heat the oil in a deep-fat fryer, wok, or large, heavy-based saucepan to 350°–375°F, or until a cube of bread browns in 30 seconds. Cook the bonda in batches: Dip the potato balls in the batter and carefully drop them into the hot oil one by one, making sure that the pan is not overcrowded. Deep-fry for 3–4 minutes or until golden, then remove with a slotted spoon and drain on paper towels. Serve hot.

steamed rice and vegetable dumplings

These savory dumplings, called *kozhukatta*, can be eaten as a snack at any time of the day, with a chutney or pickle. Or serve with a drizzle of spiced oil, made by frying curry leaves, dried, hot red chili pepper, mustard and coriander seeds, and a pinch of hot chili powder in oil until sizzling.

MAKES 12

about 2 cups rice flour

1 tablespoon vegetable oil, plus extra for
   brushing

sea salt and freshly ground black pepper

FOR THE FILLING:

2 tablespoons vegetable oil

1 teaspoon mustard seeds

1/4 cup minced onion

1 teaspoon ground coriander

1/2 teaspoon hot chili powder

1/2 teaspoon ground turmeric

2 tablespoons chopped tomatoes

1/4 cup green peas

1 Put the rice flour and a little salt in a large bowl and make a well in the center. Gradually stir in 3/4–1 cup warm water or just enough to make a smooth dough. Add the oil and mix to a soft dough, adding a little more flour or water if necessary.

2 For the filling, heat the oil in a large pan, add the mustard seeds, and, as they start to pop, add the onion and a little salt. Cook for 5 minutes or until the onion is soft. Add the coriander, chili powder, and turmeric, and mix well. Add the tomatoes and 1/4 cup water, and cook for 2 minutes. Stir in the peas and 1 teaspoon pepper. Cover and simmer gently for 10–15 minutes. Remove from the heat.

3 Oil your hands. Break off a piece of dough about the size of a golf ball and shape into a flat patty. Place a small spoonful of the filling in the middle of the patty and lightly fold the dough around it to enclose. Gently roll into a ball and set aside on a plate. Repeat to use all the dough and filling.

4 Set a steamer over a large pan of water and bring to a boil. Put the dumplings in the steamer, cover, and steam for 15 minutes or until the dough is cooked through. Serve hot or cold.

samosas

From humble beginnings in Punjabi homes and small *dhabas* (street cafés), samosas have become known the world over and were one of the first Indian foods to be sold ready-cooked in supermarkets. Making them at home with bought samosa pastry is easy, however, and allows greater flexibility with fillings. If samosa pastry isn't available, use phyllo instead. Each of the featured recipes is enough to fill 9 oz pastry, to serve 4.

Simply cut the samosa pastry into strips, that are 10 by 3 inches. Place 1 heaped tablespoon of filling in the middle at one end of a pastry strip. Fold a corner of the pastry over the filling to form a triangle, then continue folding in alternate directions along the strip to make a triangular parcel.

Two-thirds fill a deep-fat fryer, heavy-based saucepan, or wok with vegetable oil and heat to 350°–375°F. Fry your samosas, one at a time, for 2–3 minutes until golden. Drain on paper towels, and serve hot or cold.

▲ green bean and pea filling

Heat 4 tbsp oil in a pan. Add 1 tsp mustard seeds and, when they start to pop, add 2 diced onions and fry until soft. Add 1 tsp ground coriander, 1 tsp hot chili powder, ½ tsp garam masala, ½ tsp ground turmeric, and a little salt. Fry for 1 minute, then add 2 diced potatoes, 1 diced carrot, 1 cup diced green beans, and 1 cup green peas. Cover and cook for 15 minutes. Remove from the heat and set aside to cool.

spicy potato filling

Boil 2 cups cubed potatoes until tender; drain and mash lightly. Heat 4 tbsp oil in a frying pan and sauté 3 minced medium-hot green chili peppers, 1 tsp shredded ginger, and a pinch of cumin seeds for 1 minute. Add 1 minced onion and cook until soft. Add 1 tsp ground coriander, 1/2 tsp each garam masala and turmeric, and a little salt. Cook for 2 minutes. Add the potatoes and 1/4 cup chopped cilantro. Cool before using.

spiced lamb filling

Heat 5 tbsp oil in a pan and fry 3 chopped onions until soft and golden. Add 2 chopped tomatoes, 2 minced medium-hot green chili peppers, 2 chopped garlic cloves, 1 tsp each hot chili powder, garam masala, and tomato paste, and a little salt; mix well. Add 1 cup water and bring to a boil. Stir in 2/3 cup cubed potatoes and 1 cup ground lamb. Simmer, covered, for 20 minutes or until the mixture is well cooked and thick. Stir in 3 tbsp chopped cilantro and set aside to cool.

▲ vegetable and cashew nut filling

Boil 2 cubed potatoes in salted water for 5 minutes. Add 1/2 cup chopped cauliflower and cook for 2–3 minutes; drain. Heat 3 tbsp oil in a frying pan and fry 2 finely sliced onions, 2 minced medium-hot green chili peppers, and 1/2 cup broken cashew nuts for 4 minutes. Stir in 1/2 tsp each turmeric and garam masala. Add the potato mixture, 3 cups finely sliced mushrooms, and 2 cups spinach. Cook, covered, for 4 minutes; the vegetables should be slightly crunchy. Stir in 1/4 cup chopped cilantro and let cool.

beet cutlets

You may associate cutlets with meat such as veal, but it is a different story in India where they are savory cakes. The first time I ate beet cutlets was at a wedding engagement in a Christian friend's home, so I assumed it was a Christian specialty of our region. However, later in the week I had the same cutlet at Kumar's bakery in our town with a cup of tea. I then realized it was a new fashion in snack foods. The beet flavor was fascinating to me because I had only seen the vegetable used in curry dishes. Mr. Kumar was kind enough to give me his recipe and I have subsequently made it many times.

MAKES 6

8 tablespoons vegetable oil

1 teaspoon mustard seeds

few curry leaves

1-inch piece fresh ginger, peeled and finely sliced

1 onion, peeled and finely sliced

1 teaspoon ground turmeric

1 teaspoon hot chili powder

1 teaspoon garam masala

1 cup cooked, peeled, and finely diced beets

$2/3$ cup peeled and finely diced potato

$1/3$ cup green peas

$1/2$ cup milk

4 cups fine, dry bread crumbs

sea salt

1 Heat 4 tablespoons oil in a large frying pan. Add the mustard seeds and, when they start to pop, add the curry leaves, ginger, and onion. Fry for 5 minutes or until the onion is soft.

2 Stir in the turmeric, chili powder, and garam masala. Stir in the beets, potatoes, and peas, then add about $1/2$ cup water and a little salt. Cook for 10 minutes or until the vegetables are very tender. Remove the pan from the heat and set aside to cool.

3 When the vegetable mixture is cool enough to handle, divide into 6 equal portions and form into teardrop-shapes.

4 Pour the milk into a shallow dish and spread the bread crumbs out on a plate. Dip each beet cutlet into the milk, then into the bread crumbs, turning to coat evenly and gently pressing the crumbs onto the cutlets to adhere.

5 Heat the remaining oil in a clean frying pan. You may need to cook the cutlets in two batches. Add them to the hot pan and fry for 3–5 minutes until crisp and golden, turning frequently. Drain on paper towels. Serve the cutlets hot, with kiwi fruit chutney (page 30) or date chutney (page 31).

garlic and chili pickle

Garlic and chili are common ingredients in Indian cooking, but combining the two to make a pickle was chef Ramanathan's idea. He opened one of the first Indian restaurants in Britain. Sadly, he passed away a few years ago, but the memory of his lovely pickle lingers on. It took me a while to discover how to make it, and even longer to make it taste like his.

SERVES 8

4 tablespoons vegetable oil
pinch of fenugreek seeds
1/2 cup peeled and sliced garlic cloves
1 teaspoon tomato paste
1 teaspoon crushed mustard seeds
1 teaspoon hot chili powder
1/2 teaspoon ground turmeric
4 medium-hot green chili peppers, chopped
1 cup white vinegar
1 teaspoon brown sugar
sea salt

1   Heat the oil in a large, nonstick frying pan. Add the fenugreek seeds and cook, stirring constantly, for 1 minute or until they turn golden. Add the garlic and cook gently, stirring occasionally, for about 5 minutes until it is tender and has started to color.

2   Add the tomato paste, mustard seeds, chili powder, turmeric, chilies, and a little salt. Fry the mixture for 2–3 minutes, then pour in the vinegar and cook over a low heat for 25–30 minutes until the garlic is browned and all the liquid has evaporated.

3   Stir in the sugar, then remove the pan from the heat and set aside to cool before use or storage. You can keep the pickle in a covered jar in the fridge for up to 2 weeks.

shrimp pickle

This recipe is a contribution from a fishing family living in Cochin, South India, where fresh seafood is eaten at least twice a day. The people of Cochin are said to make the best fish dishes in the world, slipping their fresh catch of the day straight into the pan along with traditional smoky tamarind and sun-dried, hot red chili peppers. The pickle was devised as a means of survival during the monsoon and other rough times when fishermen were unable to put their boats out to sea.

SERVES 4

1/2-inch piece fresh ginger, peeled and chopped
2 garlic cloves, peeled
1/2 teaspoon ground turmeric
1 teaspoon sea salt
7 oz peeled small shrimp, chopped

vegetable oil for deep-frying, plus 4 tablespoons
1/2 teaspoon mustard seeds
few curry leaves
2 medium-hot green chili peppers, slit lengthwise
1 teaspoon hot chili powder
1 teaspoon mustard powder
1 1/4 cups white wine vinegar

1   Using a small spice mill, or a mortar and pestle, pound the chopped ginger and garlic together to make a paste. Set aside.

2   In a small bowl, mix together the turmeric and salt with 1 tablespoon water to make a paste. Add the chopped shrimp and stir to coat.

3   Heat a 2-inch depth of oil in a large, heavy-based saucepan or wok to 350°–375°F, or until a cube of bread browns in 30 seconds. Deep-fry the shrimp for 3–4 minutes until light golden, then remove with a slotted spoon and set aside to drain on paper towels.

4   Heat 4 tablespoons oil in a large frying pan. Add the mustard seeds and, when they start to pop, add the curry leaves, chilies, chili powder, mustard powder, and the ginger-garlic paste. Cook, stirring constantly, for 1 minute, or until the spices give off a toasted aroma.

5   Add the shrimp and cook, stirring constantly, for 2–3 minutes longer or until all the pieces are coated with the spice mixture. Pour in the wine vinegar and simmer, stirring occasionally, for 10 minutes or until the pickle thickens. Remove the pan from the heat and set aside to cool before serving.

coconut chutney

There is nothing like a freshly made, tangy, spiced chutney to accompany special snacks, curries, and rice dishes. Made with fresh coconut, this chutney has a good, sharp, clean flavor.

SERVES 4

1 tablespoon tamarind pulp

1¼ cups freshly grated coconut

2 medium-hot green chili peppers, chopped

1-inch piece fresh ginger, peeled and
   sliced

1 garlic clove, peeled

2 tablespoons vegetable oil

1 teaspoon mustard seeds

1 small onion, peeled and minced

10 curry leaves

sea salt

1 Break up the tamarind pulp and place in a small bowl. Add 3 tablespoons hot water and let soak for 20–30 minutes. Press the mixture through a strainer to extract 3 tablespoons of tamarind liquid, and pour this into a blender. Add the coconut, chilies, ginger, garlic, and a little salt, and process to a smooth paste.

2 Heat the oil in a small frying pan. Add the mustard seeds and, when they start to pop, stir in the onion and curry leaves. Cook over a medium heat for 2–3 minutes or until the onion is golden. Lower the heat and add the coconut mixture. Mix well and serve hot or cold.

kiwi fruit chutney

As I adore fresh chutneys, I enjoy experimenting with different fruits and vegetables to extend my repertoire. Kiwi fruit, with its sweet-sour flavor, has the ideal qualities for a delicious chutney. Try this recipe with other fruits, too.

SERVES 4

7 oz kiwi fruit

1 tomato, minced

2 medium-hot green chili peppers, chopped

3 shallots, peeled and chopped

½-inch piece fresh ginger, peeled and
   minced

pinch of freshly ground black pepper

sea salt

1 Peel the kiwi fruit and cut the flesh into small pieces. Place the tomato, chilies, shallots, ginger, black pepper, and a little salt in a blender and pulse briefly until the tomatoes are just lightly crushed.

2 Add the kiwi fruit a little at a time, processing slowly until you have a coarse-textured chutney. Transfer to a small serving dish.

sweet mango chutney

Made with sweet fruit, this versatile chutney is reminiscent of Bombay and other areas of the Maharashtra state. It tastes very different from the spicy, sour mango chutneys that are typical of my home state, Kerala.

SERVES 4

7 oz sweet mango
2 tablespoons chopped shallot or onion
2 medium-hot green chili peppers, chopped
2 garlic cloves, peeled
2 tablespoons curry leaves
sea salt

1 Peel the mango. Cut the flesh away from the pit, then dice it and set aside. Place the shallot or onion, chilies, garlic, curry leaves, and a little salt in a blender and process to a smooth paste. Add the diced mango and process to a coarse paste.

2 Transfer the mango chutney to a serving bowl, cover with plastic wrap, and chill before serving.

date chutney

Dates make a good, rich chutney that goes particularly well with samosas (pages 24–5) and onion bhajis (page 20). Using fresh, juicy dates rather than dried ones gives a truly succulent dip.

SERVES 4

7 oz fresh pitted dates, chopped
3 garlic cloves, peeled and chopped
2 dried, hot red chili peppers
¹⁄₄ cup lime juice
2 tablespoons freshly grated coconut
sea salt

1 Place the dates, garlic, chilies, lime juice, and coconut in a blender and process to a smooth paste. Transfer to a serving bowl.

2 soups, salads, and side dishes

Keralan seafood soup

This exquisite soup combines three things Kerala is particularly renowned for—spices, coconuts, and seafood—and it can be varied to include any fresh seafood. It is rich in flavor, and makes a substantial dish thanks to the inclusion of rice. Jamie Oliver says it's one of the best soups he has ever had in his life. I recommend you serve it with bread, preferably appams (pages 158–9) or parathas (pages 155–6).

SERVES 4

1/3 cup long-grain white rice

4 tablespoons vegetable oil

1 teaspoon mustard seeds

pinch of cumin seeds

20 curry leaves, chopped

4 garlic cloves, peeled and chopped

1-inch piece fresh ginger, peeled and
  chopped

3 medium-hot green chili peppers, finely sliced

3 onions, peeled and chopped

1/2 teaspoon ground turmeric

1/2 teaspoon hot chili powder

1/2 teaspoon crushed black pepper

9 oz raw shrimp, peeled, deveined, and
  halved if large

1 cup coconut milk

FOR SERVING:

4 cooked king or tiger shrimp in shell (optional)

3 tablespoons freshly grated coconut

1 Cook the rice in 1 1/2 cups water in a small saucepan. When the rice is just tender, drain, reserving 1 cup of the cooking water. Set aside.

2 Heat the oil in a medium saucepan. Add the mustard seeds and, when they start to pop, add the cumin seeds, curry leaves, garlic, ginger, chilies, and onions. Fry for 5 minutes or until the onions are soft. Stir in the turmeric, chili powder, and black pepper, and stir-fry for 2 minutes.

3 Add the shrimp, cooked rice, and reserved cooking water. Cook over a low heat for 10 minutes or until the shrimp are cooked and the soup is creamy. Add the coconut milk and bring to a boil, then lower the heat and simmer for 5 minutes longer.

4 Ladle the seafood soup into warmed bowls and top each serving with a whole cooked shrimp, if desired. Scatter with freshly grated coconut and serve.

spiced lentil soup

Soups aren't something you come across very often in India, as they're not part of the traditional food culture, but increasingly they are offered as a first course on restaurant menus. This one is based on a spiced mixture of lentils and beans, and is the ideal winter warmer. Green bell pepper and spinach help make it colorful, and you can add potatoes to make it more filling, if desired.

SERVES 4

²/₃ *cup dried split red lentils*

¹/₃ *cup dried chana dal, or yellow split peas*

¹/₃ *cup dried mung beans*

1 onion, peeled and finely sliced

1 tomato, diced

1 green bell pepper, cored, seeded, and diced

¹/₂ *cup spinach leaves, tough stems removed*

4 garlic cloves, peeled and minced

2 medium-hot green chili peppers, finely sliced

1-inch piece fresh ginger, peeled and minced

1 teaspoon hot chili powder

1 teaspoon garam masala

1 teaspoon ground turmeric

sea salt

¹/₄ *cup minced cilantro for garnish*

1 Combine all the ingredients, except the cilantro, in a saucepan. Stir in 5 cups water and bring to a boil. Simmer, stirring frequently, for 20 minutes or until the lentils and beans are thoroughly cooked.

2 Ladle the soup into warmed bowls and sprinkle minced cilantro over each portion. Serve hot, with Indian bread, if desired.

spicy mixed salad

Just like anywhere else in the world, salads are popular in India, but they are usually spiked with some chili. This recipe is very flexible—vary the spices, vegetables, and fruit to taste.

SERVES 4

3 tomatoes

1/2 hothouse cucumber

2 apples

2 pears

2 oranges

2 bananas, peeled

1/3 cup quartered radishes

pinch of garam masala

1 1/2 teaspoons sea salt

1/2 teaspoon hot chili powder

2 tablespoons lemon juice

1 Cut the tomatoes, cucumber, apples, and pears into bite-sized chunks and place in a large bowl. Peel and segment the oranges, then halve each segment and add to the bowl. Cut the bananas into chunks and toss them into the salad with the quartered radishes.

2 Sprinkle the garam masala, salt, and chili powder over the salad, then add the lemon juice and toss well. Cover and chill slightly before serving.

papaya salad

In India, the tropical papaya is included in curries, stir-fries, and dishes such as this salad, which has a refreshing, sweet-tangy combination of ingredients.

SERVES 4

1 small, ripe papaya

1 guava

1 tablespoon vegetable oil

1/2 teaspoon dried urad dal

8 shallots, peeled and finely sliced

pinch of hot chili powder

1/4 cup wine or cider vinegar

pinch of sea salt

5 tablespoons coconut milk

juice of 1 lemon

1 Peel, halve, and seed the papaya and guava, then cut into cubes. Set aside in a large bowl.

2 Heat the oil in a frying pan. Add the urad dal and fry, stirring, for 1–2 minutes until it turns brown, then add the shallots and sauté over a low heat for 1 minute. Sprinkle in the chili powder, then add the vinegar and salt. Increase the heat and stir-fry for 1 minute. Remove the pan from the heat and slowly mix in the coconut milk.

3 Pour the shallot mixture over the prepared fruits, add the lemon juice, and toss well. Serve cold.

coconut and radish salad

This salad is wonderfully quick to make and has a lovely clean, fresh flavor, with a nutty crunch provided by the toasted urad dal. You can use cucumber instead of radishes, if you prefer.

SERVES 4

2 tablespoons vegetable oil
1 teaspoon mustard seeds
1 teaspoon dried urad dal
few curry leaves
4 oz shallots, peeled and halved
3 medium-hot green chili peppers, minced
3 tablespoons lemon juice
3 tablespoons white wine vinegar
1/2 cup freshly grated coconut
8 oz radishes, quartered
sea salt

1   Heat the oil in a large frying pan or wok. Add the mustard seeds and, when they start to pop, add the urad dal and curry leaves. Cook, stirring constantly, for 1–2 minutes until the urad dal turns brown.

2   Add the shallots and stir-fry for 5 minutes or until they are shiny and translucent. Add the chilies and a little salt, and stir-fry for 1 minute. Pour in the lemon juice and vinegar, then add the grated coconut and mix well. Remove the pan from the heat.

3   Transfer the fried mixture to a large bowl. Add the quartered radishes and toss to mix, then serve.

tomato and red onion raita

In India, I knew raita simply as an accompaniment to *Hyderabadi biryani*, but since moving to London, I have realized that it is a very important item on every Indian restaurant menu. Raita helps cool the effect of those fiery dishes that can take you by surprise, so many British people order it as a matter of routine when having an Indian meal. Red onions work fine in such a dish, because they are milder and sweeter than ordinary onions.

SERVES 4

1/2-inch piece fresh ginger

3 medium-hot green chili peppers

1 red onion, peeled

1 tomato

2-oz piece hothouse cucumber

1 cup plain yogurt

FOR SERVING:

pinch of hot chili powder

chopped cilantro (optional)

1   Peel and mince the ginger. The easiest way to do this is to remove the skin with a swivel vegetable peeler, then cut the ginger into thin slices. Cut these slices into matchsticks, then into tiny dice.

2   Finely slice the green chili into rings. Mince the red onion. Cut the tomato and cucumber into tiny cubes, discarding the seeds.

3   Put the yogurt in a large bowl. Add the tomato, cucumber, red onion, chilies, and ginger, and stir to mix. Serve sprinkled with a pinch of chili powder and chopped cilantro, if desired.

thoran

Thorans are lightly cooked vegetable salads. They appear at nearly every Keralan meal, providing a fresh-tasting, crunchy contrast to sauced dishes (we often describe thorans as "dry" dishes). Thorans' unique mild and nutty flavors are derived from fried urad dal, curry leaves, and freshly grated coconut—the most important ingredient. Onion or shallot is usually included, and sometimes cashew nuts for extra crunch.

The basic thoran cooking technique is reminiscent of Chinese stir-frying. It suits most firm vegetables, but thorans can also be made with tougher leafy greens, such as cabbage, and starchy foods like cooked legumes, potato, and plantain. In Kerala, we use whatever vegetables are in season. The vegetables may be par-cooked before stir-frying, but most often they are cut into small pieces and added straight to the pan. Each of the following thorans will serve 4–6. Serve them hot and freshly made.

▲ shallot thoran

Heat 5 tbsp oil in a pan. Add 1 tsp mustard seeds and, when they start to pop, add 1 tsp dried urad dal and 10 curry leaves. Cook, stirring, for 1–2 minutes or until the dal turns brown. Add 2 cups minced shallots, 3 minced medium-hot green chili peppers, and a little salt, and cook for 5 minutes or until the shallots are translucent. Mix in 1 cup freshly grated coconut and a few extra curry leaves, and stir-fry for 1 minute.

white cabbage thoran

Heat 5 tbsp oil in a pan. Fry 1½ tbsp mustard seeds until they pop. Add 10 curry leaves and 1 tsp urad dal. Cook, stirring, for 1–2 minutes until the dal browns. Add 3 finely sliced onions and 4 dried, hot red chili peppers. Cook on a high heat for 1 minute, then gently until the onions are soft. Add salt and 1 tsp turmeric. Stir in 1 small head shredded cabbage; cook, covered, for 15 minutes. Stir in 1 cup freshly grated coconut.

green bean thoran

Heat 5 tbsp oil in a pan. Fry 1 tsp mustard seeds until they pop. Add 10 curry leaves and 1 tsp dried urad dal. Cook, stirring, for 1–2 minutes until the dal turns brown. Add 1 finely sliced small onion and 2 diced medium-hot green chili peppers. Cook on a high heat for 1 minute, then lower the heat and cook for 5 minutes longer. Stir in 1 tsp turmeric and a little salt. Add 2 cups chopped green beans and cook, covered, for 15–20 minutes until tender. Stir in ½ cup freshly grated coconut.

▲ Savoy cabbage and carrot thoran

Pound 2 medium-hot green chili peppers, 1 tbsp chopped ginger, and 3 garlic cloves with 1 tomato. Heat 5 tbsp oil in a pan and fry 1 tsp mustard seeds until they pop. Add 1 tsp dried urad dal; cook, stirring, until brown. Add 2 finely sliced onions and 10 curry leaves; cook until soft. Add the chili paste; stir 1 minute. Add 2 shredded carrots, 5 cups shredded Savoy cabbage, and 3 tbsp water. Cover and cook for 10 minutes. Stir in 2 cups freshly grated coconut and cook for 2 minutes.

okra masala

Widely known as bhindi or ladies' fingers, okra is a favorite vegetable in India, prized for its unusual flavor and texture, whether it is cooked in a tomato and onion masala in the Northern style, as in this recipe, or in a crunchy South Indian thoran. You have to be careful when using okra because it doesn't handle heat well and so needs to be cooked briefly. Choose relatively small specimens as large ones tend to have large seeds and can be very stringy, even after cooking. I love to eat this okra masala with two chapattis (page 154)—a perfect dinner for me. You can, of course, serve it with other Indian breads, or toasted poppadoms, if you prefer. *Illustrated on previous page*

SERVES 4

3 tablespoons vegetable oil
pinch of fenugreek seeds
pinch of fennel seeds
2–3 cardamom pods
1-inch piece cinnamon stick
1 bay leaf
3 garlic cloves, peeled and chopped
3 onions, peeled and minced
1/2 teaspoon ground turmeric
1/2 teaspoon hot chili powder
1 teaspoon ground coriander
1 teaspoon tomato paste
2 tomatoes, finely diced
8 oz okra
cilantro leaves for garnish

1 Heat the oil in a medium saucepan, karahi, or wok. Add the fenugreek seeds, fennel seeds, cardamom pods, cinnamon stick, bay leaf, garlic, and onions, and cook, stirring occasionally, for about 10 minutes until the onions are golden.

2 Add the turmeric, chili powder, ground coriander, and tomato paste. Stir well and cook for 1 more minute. Add the diced tomatoes and 2 1/2 cups water, then bring to a boil. Simmer for 10 minutes or until the sauce is thick.

3 Meanwhile, trim the ends of the okra and cut into 1/2-inch pieces. Stir the okra into the masala sauce, then cover and cook over a low heat for 5 minutes or until the okra is tender. Serve garnished with cilantro leaves.

eggplant stir-fry

Eggplant is considered a highly versatile vegetable in India, and is available in an amazing array of colors, sizes, and flavors. This is an easy way to enhance it, and uses just a few ingredients.

SERVES 4
4 tablespoons vegetable oil
1 teaspoon mustard seeds
1 onion, peeled and thinly sliced
few curry leaves
1 medium-hot green chili pepper, slit lengthwise
1 lb eggplants, cubed (about 6 cups)

1   Heat the oil in a large frying pan or wok. Add the mustard seeds and, when they start to pop, add the onion and curry leaves. Cook for 5 minutes or until the onion is soft.

2   Add the chili and eggplant cubes, and stir well. Cover and cook gently for 5 minutes, then remove the lid and stir-fry for 5 minutes or until the eggplant is tender. Serve hot.

green bean stir-fry

A speedy, light side dish such as this one is an excellent way to add a healthy component to a rich curry meal. You can use any variety of green bean—choose whichever looks freshest.

SERVES 4
9 oz green beans, trimmed
2 tablespoons vegetable oil
1 teaspoon mustard seeds
2 onions, peeled and minced
few curry leaves
3 medium-hot green chili peppers, slit lengthwise
large pinch of ground turmeric
sea salt

1   Cut the beans into 1-inch pieces. Heat the oil in a large frying pan or wok and fry the mustard seeds until they start to pop. Add the onions and curry leaves, and cook for 4–5 minutes or until the onions are soft. Add the chilies, turmeric, and a little salt, and sauté for 1 minute.

2   Add the beans and sprinkle in a few tablespoons of water, then cover and cook for 5 minutes or until just tender. Remove the lid and stir-fry for 5 minutes or until dry and crunchy. Serve hot.

green pepper stir-fry

I was introduced to bell peppers in North India, where they are known as *shimla mirch*. The region has some unforgettable dishes based on them. Peppers bring a lot of color to dishes, whether they are used raw or grilled, or made into a stir-fry such as this one. Tomatoes and onions are included here, and the result is an ideal accompaniment for sauced dishes.

SERVES 4

11 oz green bell peppers
4 tablespoons vegetable oil
1/2 teaspoon cumin seeds
2 onions, peeled and finely sliced
2 medium-hot green chili peppers, slit
  lengthwise
1-inch piece fresh ginger, peeled and
  finely sliced
1/2 teaspoon ground turmeric
1 teaspoon ground coriander
2 tomatoes, finely diced
2 tablespoons minced cilantro for garnish

1 Halve, core, and seed the green bell peppers, then slice into long, thin strips. Heat the oil in a large frying pan or wok. Add the cumin seeds and then the onions, chilies, and ginger. Cook, stirring occasionally, for 5 minutes or until the onions are soft.

2 Add the turmeric and ground coriander, and cook for 1 more minute before adding the tomatoes. Stir well, then add the green bell peppers. Sprinkle a few tablespoons of water over the ingredients in the pan and cook for 5 minutes, stirring constantly, until the peppers are soft.

3 Transfer to a large serving dish, sprinkle with the cilantro, and serve hot.

baby corn and carrot stir-fry

Last year I started cooking daily for my colleagues because I wanted to encourage them to eat healthily. One day, as I was shopping in the supermarket, I was drawn to the display of baby vegetables and realized that they could be combined to make the perfect crunchy vegetable side dish. Everyone loves this recipe and, since its inception, there is not another dish that I have prepared as often.

SERVES 4

4 oz baby corn

4 oz baby carrots

2 tablespoons vegetable oil

2 onions, peeled and sliced lengthwise

1-inch piece fresh ginger, peeled and finely shredded

2 garlic cloves, peeled and chopped

1/2 teaspoon ground turmeric

1/2 teaspoon hot chili powder

1/2 teaspoon garam masala

sea salt

2 tablespoons chopped cilantro for garnish

1 Cut the baby corn lengthwise into quarters. Halve the baby carrots lengthwise. Set aside.

2 Heat the oil in a large frying pan. Add the onions, ginger, and garlic, and cook, stirring occasionally, for 5 minutes or until the onions are golden brown.

3 Add the turmeric, chili powder, and garam masala, and cook, stirring, for a further minute. Stir in the baby corn and carrots, then sprinkle with a few tablespoons of water and add a pinch of salt. Cook for 5 minutes: the vegetables should be cooked but still crunchy.

4 Remove the pan from the heat. Sprinkle the cilantro over the stir-fry and serve.

spicy new potatoes with spinach

During the new potato season, my wife, Alison, insisted that I make her a spicy dish with baby new potatoes. I agreed on one condition: that I would be able to add my favorite vegetable, spinach, to it. We both loved the combination.

SERVES 4

12 oz small or medium new potatoes
2 teaspoons ground turmeric
2 tablespoons vegetable oil
1 teaspoon mustard seeds
1 teaspoon dried urad dal
1-inch piece fresh ginger, peeled and minced
1 medium-hot green chili pepper, sliced

1 large onion, peeled and chopped
1 teaspoon hot chili powder
2 tomatoes, chopped
9 oz baby leaf spinach (about 2¹/₂ cups)
juice of ¹/₂ lemon
sea salt

1 Place the new potatoes in a large saucepan, cover generously with water, and add ¹/₂ teaspoon turmeric and a little salt. Bring to a boil, then cover and cook for 15 minutes or until the potatoes are tender. Drain and set aside.

2 Heat the oil in a large frying pan. Add the mustard seeds and, when they start to pop, add the urad dal, ginger, and chili. Stir-fry for 30 seconds. Add the onion and continue stir-frying until it is softened and light golden. Mix in the chili powder, the remaining turmeric, and a little salt, and stir-fry for 1 more minute.

3 Add the tomatoes and cook, stirring constantly, for 5 minutes or until they break down. Cover the pan and cook for 2 minutes longer, stirring frequently.

4 Add the spinach and cook, stirring constantly, for 5 minutes or until wilted. Lower the heat, add the drained potatoes and lemon juice, and stir thoroughly to combine. Serve hot.

spinach and coconut

This is a re-creation of my mother's best spinach dish, which she used to make with a red leaf variety. You won't believe the difference freshly grated coconut and green chilies make to spinach. Use as much coconut as you like—the taste will only get better. I like to eat this with plain boiled rice and my yogurt curry sauce, the basic moru kachiathu (page 89).

SERVES 4

1 cup freshly grated coconut
3 medium-hot green chili peppers, chopped
4 tablespoons vegetable oil
1 teaspoon mustard seeds
1 teaspoon dried urad dal
10 curry leaves
2 onions, peeled and minced
1 teaspoon ground turmeric
11 oz spinach leaves, chopped (about 5 cups)
sea salt

1 Place the grated coconut and chopped green chilies in a blender with 1 cup water, and process to a coarse paste. Set aside.

2 Heat the oil in a medium saucepan or wok. Add the mustard seeds and, when they start to pop, add the urad dal and curry leaves. Stir-fry for 1–2 minutes or until the urad dal turns brown. Add the onions and stir-fry for 5 minutes or until soft.

3 Stir in the turmeric and a little salt and mix well, then add the chopped spinach leaves. Cover and cook for 5 minutes. Add the coconut paste and stir well. Lower the heat and cook gently for 5 minutes longer, stirring occasionally. Serve hot.

stuffed peppers

White radish isn't very common in India, but I find the combination of strong-flavored white radish and sweet-tasting bell peppers excellent. Chick peas help to make this a substantial side dish that can be served with Malabar parathas (page 155) as a healthy lunch or light supper. For an attractive appetizer, use a selection of different colored peppers.

SERVES 6

3 bell peppers

FOR THE STUFFING:
3 tablespoons vegetable oil
1/2 teaspoon cumin seeds
2 garlic cloves, peeled and chopped
2 onions, peeled and minced
1/4 teaspoon ground turmeric

1/2 teaspoon hot chili powder
1/2 teaspoon garam masala
1 1/4 cups thinly sliced white radish (daikon)
1 cup drained, canned chick peas (garbanzo beans)
2 tomatoes, finely diced
2 tablespoons chopped cilantro
sea salt

1 Preheat the oven to 400°F. Carefully slice off the tops of the bell peppers and reserve to use as lids. Scrape out the seeds from the pepper cavities. Use 1 tablespoon oil to grease a small baking dish that will hold the peppers standing upright.

2 Heat 2 tablespoons oil in a large frying pan, karahi, or wok. Add the cumin seeds, garlic, and onions, and fry for 5 minutes or until the onions are soft. Sprinkle in the turmeric, chili powder, garam masala, and a little salt, and stir well.

3 Add the radishes, chick peas, and tomatoes, and cook for 5 minutes, stirring frequently. Remove the pan from the heat and let cool slightly.

4 Fill the pepper cavities with the radish and chick pea mixture and replace the tops. Place the peppers upright in the oiled baking dish. Sprinkle with 3 tablespoons of water and bake for 20 minutes or until the peppers are tender.

5 Carefully remove the lids from the peppers and sprinkle with the cilantro. Serve hot, halving the peppers lengthwise as you serve them.

3 legumes, cheese, and eggs

mung bean curry

This dish is popular with the agricultural community of Kerala, and is regularly served at lunchtime with a dish of watery rice. It satisfies the hungry farmer after a hard morning's work in the sun and it's a good source of water. We also serve mung bean curry for breakfast with steamed rice cakes. You can vary this dish by adding green bananas instead of potatoes.

SERVES 4

1¹/₂ cups freshly grated coconut
2 medium-hot green chili peppers
1¹/₂ cups dried mung beans
1 teaspoon hot chili powder
¹/₂ teaspoon ground turmeric
2 potatoes, peeled and diced
4 tablespoons vegetable oil
1 teaspoon mustard seeds
few curry leaves
3 dried, hot red chili peppers

1 Place the coconut, green chilies, and 1 cup water in a blender and process to a coarse paste. Set aside.

2 Put the mung beans in a saucepan with 3 cups water. Add the chili powder and turmeric, and bring to a boil, then cover and cook for 20 minutes. Mix in the diced potatoes and continue simmering for 10–12 minutes longer or until the beans and potatoes are cooked.

3 Lower the heat and add the coconut and chili paste. Stir well, then simmer for a few more minutes over a low heat.

4 Meanwhile, heat the oil in a small frying pan. Add the mustard seeds and, when they start to pop, add the curry leaves and the dried red chilies. Pour the contents of the pan over the cooked mung beans, toss well, and serve hot.

spinach and chick pea curry

Chick pea dishes are common in North India, where this legume is a local crop and available in a surprising array of colors and shapes. The strong flavor of garam masala complements the rich taste of chick peas exceptionally well, and spinach imparts color and flavor. You can serve this curry with any Indian bread.

SERVES 4

1 medium-hot green chili pepper, seeded and
   chopped
1-inch piece fresh ginger, peeled and minced
2 tablespoons vegetable oil
2 garlic cloves, peeled and sliced
1 onion, peeled and minced
1/4 teaspoon hot chili powder

1/4 teaspoon ground turmeric
1/2 teaspoon ground coriander
2 teaspoons tomato paste
1 lb spinach leaves, tough stems removed
14 oz canned chick peas (garbanzo beans),
   drained and rinsed
sea salt

1 Using a pestle and mortar, finely grind the chili and ginger together, adding a spoonful of water to help make a paste. Set aside.

2 Heat the oil in a large frying pan. Add the garlic and stir-fry for 30 seconds, then add the onion and cook, stirring constantly, for about 5 minutes until it is soft and lightly golden at the edges. Add the chili powder, turmeric, ground coriander, chili-ginger paste, and tomato paste, and stir-fry for 2 minutes.

3 Pour 1 1/4 cups water into the pan and bring to a boil. Stir in the spinach and chick peas, along with a pinch of salt. Cook, stirring occasionally, for 5 minutes or until they are well blended with the spices and the spinach has wilted. Serve hot.

chick pea curry

A Punjabi friend from Delhi gave me the idea for this recipe. Keralans are used to eating chick pea curries with roasted coconut sauce, but here I have tried to combine North and South Indian styles to create a unique flavor. The strong flavor of the spice blend, married with the creamy texture of coconut milk, makes it rather like a masala sauce. It is best served with a mild side dish.

SERVES 4–6

4 tablespoons vegetable oil

1-inch piece cinnamon stick

2 whole cloves

3 cardamom pods, crushed

pinch of fennel seeds

4 garlic cloves, peeled and chopped

1-inch piece fresh ginger, minced

2 medium-hot green chili peppers, minced

3 onions, peeled and chopped

$^1/_2$ teaspoon ground turmeric

1 teaspoon hot chili powder

1$^1/_2$ teaspoons ground coriander

$^1/_2$ teaspoon garam masala

1 teaspoon tomato paste

4 tomatoes, chopped

28 oz canned chick peas (garbanzo beans), drained and rinsed

1 cup coconut milk

sea salt

$^1/_4$ cup chopped cilantro for garnish

1 Heat the oil in a saucepan. Add the cinnamon stick, cloves, cardamoms, fennel seeds, garlic, ginger, and chilies, and sauté for 1 minute. Add the onions and fry over a medium heat for 15–20 minutes or until they are soft and golden.

2 Add the turmeric, chili powder, ground coriander, garam masala, tomato paste, and salt. Mix well, then add the chopped tomatoes and 2$^1/_2$ cups water. Bring to a boil, then add the chick peas. Cover and cook over a medium heat for 15 minutes, stirring occasionally.

3 Lower the heat and add the coconut milk. Simmer gently for 5 minutes or until the milk is well blended with the spices and chick peas. Remove the pan from the heat, sprinkle with the chopped cilantro, and serve hot.

kidney bean curry

Kidney beans are typical of North Indian states and are particularly prominent during festivals and other big occasions. Traditionally, dried beans are used, making this a time-consuming dish to prepare. Here, I simmer canned beans with spices and tomato, enriching the curry with cream before serving. You could also add spinach or potatoes to enhance the color and flavor, if desired. Serve the curry with chapattis (page 154) or Malabar parathas (page 155).

SERVES 4–6

3 tablespoons vegetable oil

1 teaspoon cumin seeds

5 garlic cloves, peeled and chopped

3 onions, peeled and sliced

1-inch piece fresh ginger, peeled and grated

1 teaspoon hot chili powder

1 teaspoon ground coriander

1 teaspoon garam masala

1/2 teaspoon ground turmeric

5 tomatoes, chopped

14 oz canned red kidney beans, drained and
  rinsed

1/4 cup heavy cream

1/3 cup chopped cilantro for garnish

1 Heat the oil in a large saucepan. Add the cumin seeds and garlic, and cook briefly until the garlic is golden. Add the onions and ginger, and cook, stirring occasionally, for 10 minutes or until the onions are softened and golden.

2 Stir in the chili powder, ground coriander, garam masala, and turmeric. Add the tomatoes and kidney beans, and cook, stirring constantly, for 1 minute. Pour in 1 3/4 cups water and bring the mixture to a boil. Lower the heat, cover, and simmer for 20 minutes or until the beans are soft.

3 Remove from the heat and stir in the cream. Garnish with the cilantro and serve.

dals

For millions of Indian people, dal—a thick, soupy dish of lentils or other legumes—is the most important dish they eat, an essential source of vegetarian protein. In North Indian villages a nutritious meal of dal and chapatti may be served at any time of day. In the South, people are more inclined to eat dal with rice. Although based on humble ingredients, dal is also served on special occasions, such as wedding feasts.

Most Indian restaurants outside of India offer only one or two dals, which often taste remarkably similar, yet on the Indian sub-continent, dals vary according to local customs, seasons, and events. Different spices and lentils are combined to give dals of varying thickness and smoothness, some mild and sweet, others hot in flavor.

The dals featured here are my favorites, inspired by those I have eaten in Delhi, and made with legumes available here. They are varied in texture and taste; each serves 4–6.

▲ lentil and spinach dal

Put ²/₃ cup dried split red lentils, ¹/₃ cup dried mung beans, ¹/₃ cup dried chana dal or split peas, 1 chopped potato, 3 diced onions, 3 diced medium-hot green chili peppers, 3 chopped tomatoes, 1 tsp turmeric, 1 tsp hot chili powder, and 2³/₄ cups water in a pan. Simmer, covered, for 15 minutes or until tender. Add 1 cup spinach leaves and cook for 5 minutes. Heat 4 tbsp oil in a pan and briefly fry ¹/₄ tsp cumin seeds with 3 minced garlic cloves, then pour this over the dal and serve.

red lentil dal

Place 1⅓ cups dried split red lentils, 2 finely sliced onions, 3 diced tomatoes, 4 minced garlic cloves, 1 tbsp minced fresh ginger, 1 tsp each hot chili powder and ground coriander, ½ tsp turmeric, salt, and 5 cups water in a pan. Simmer, covered, for 20 minutes or until tender; cook uncovered for 5 minutes. Heat 4 tbsp oil in a pan and fry 1 tsp mustard seeds until they pop. Add 10 curry leaves, stir briefly, and pour onto the dal.

mung bean and coconut dal

Work ½ cup freshly grated coconut, a pinch of cumin seeds, and 1 cup water to a paste in a blender. Place 1 heaped cup dried mung beans in a pan with 5 cups water, 2 minced medium-hot green chili peppers, ½ tsp turmeric, and a little salt. Simmer, covered, for 15 minutes or until tender. Add the coconut paste and cook for 5 minutes. Lower the heat and add 1 cup coconut milk and a few curry leaves. Simmer for 5 minutes, then serve.

▲ tarka dal

Place 1⅓ cups dried split red lentils, ⅓ cup dried chana dal or split peas, 2 finely sliced onions, 2 diced tomatoes, 2 minced garlic cloves, 2 sliced medium-hot green chili peppers, 1 tsp hot chili powder, 1 tsp turmeric, salt, and 6 cups water in a pan. Simmer, covered, for 20 minutes or until the lentils are tender. Cook uncovered for 5 minutes. Heat 2 tbsp oil in a frying pan; sauté 4 shredded garlic cloves and ½ tsp cumin seeds for 1 minute. Pour onto the dal with chopped cilantro.

fried paneer with tomato and shallot chutney

Paneer dishes are now popular all over India, although they originated in the Punjab and other parts of North India. Paneer is an unusual cheese because it can be fried without a protective coating and stays firm; however, you must ensure that the oil is very hot so that the cheese colors quickly. I developed this dish to bring together the full flavor of the cheese with a refreshing shallot and tomato chutney.

SERVES 2–4

5 oz paneer cheese

vegetable oil for deep-frying

FOR THE CHUTNEY:

3 tomatoes, roughly chopped

6 shallots, peeled and roughly chopped

1 medium-hot green chili pepper, chopped

2 tablespoons cilantro leaves

1 tablespoon lemon juice

pinch of garam masala

sea salt

1 To make the chutney, put the tomatoes, shallots, chili, cilantro, and a little salt in a blender. Process briefly until the tomatoes and shallots are just crushed. Transfer the mixture to a bowl and add the lemon juice and garam masala. Set aside.

2 Cut the paneer into large cubes. Heat the oil for deep-frying in a large, heavy-based saucepan, karahi, or wok to 350°–375°F, or until a cube of bread browns in 30 seconds. Deep-fry the paneer for 1–2 minutes or until lightly browned. Remove with a slotted spoon and drain on paper towels.

3 Serve the fried paneer hot or cold, with the tomato and shallot chutney spooned over the top.

green pea and cheese curry

Famously known as *mutter paneer*, this dish appears on most Indian restaurant menus, and it's an easy dish to make. I am a big fan of it and like to eat it with Malabar parathas (page 155). You can try cooking it with green or red bell peppers, too.

SERVES 4

5 oz paneer cheese
vegetable oil for deep-frying
4 tablespoons vegetable oil
3 small onions, peeled and sliced
1-inch piece fresh ginger, peeled and minced
1 teaspoon ground coriander
1/2 teaspoon ground cumin
1/2 teaspoon ground turmeric

1/2 teaspoon garam masala
1/2 teaspoon poppy seeds
1 teaspoon tomato paste
2/3 cup green peas
1/4 cup heavy cream
3 tablespoons chopped cilantro (optional)
sea salt

1 Cut the paneer into 1/2-inch cubes. Heat the oil for deep-frying in a large, heavy-based saucepan, karahi, or wok to 350°–375°F, or until a cube of bread browns in 30 seconds. Deep-fry the paneer cubes for 1–2 minutes or until golden, then remove with a slotted spoon and set aside to drain on paper towels.

2 Heat 4 tablespoons oil in a saucepan, karahi, or wok. Add the onions and ginger, and cook, stirring occasionally, for 10 minutes until golden. Add the coriander, cumin, turmeric, garam masala, and poppy seeds, and cook for 2 minutes. Stir in the tomato paste and cook for 3–4 minutes longer.

3 Pour in 1 cup water and bring the mixture to a boil. Simmer for 5 minutes, then add the peas, fried paneer, and some salt. Cook for 5 minutes longer.

4 Turn the heat as low as possible and stir in the cream. Cook gently for 2–3 minutes before adding the cilantro, if using. Serve hot, with a flat bread.

spinach and paneer

Palak paneer, as this dish is known in North India, is one of those wholesome vegetarian dishes that is usually enjoyed by meat-eaters too. The crisp, chewy pieces of paneer go extraordinarily well with soft spiced spinach, and the creamy texture of the sauce makes it an excellent accompaniment to stronger dishes.

SERVES 4

³⁄₄ cup vegetable oil
2 oz paneer cheese, cubed
¹⁄₂ teaspoon cumin seeds
4 garlic cloves, peeled and chopped
2 onions, peeled and minced
2 medium-hot green chili peppers, minced
5 curry leaves
4 cups minced spinach leaves
1 teaspoon ground turmeric
1 teaspoon hot chili powder
1 teaspoon garam masala
1 teaspoon ground coriander
2 tomatoes, finely diced
1 green bell pepper, cored, seeded, and cubed
3¹⁄₂ tablespoons light cream
¹⁄₂ cup milk
sea salt

1 Heat ¹⁄₂ cup vegetable oil in a deep frying pan. Add the paneer cubes and cook, turning occasionally, for 1–2 minutes or until lightly browned all over. Remove the pan from the heat, lift out the paneer cubes with a slotted spoon, and set aside to drain on paper towels.

2 Heat the remaining 4 tablespoons oil in a large saucepan. Add the cumin seeds and garlic, and cook, stirring, for 1–2 minutes until golden. Add the onions, chilies, and curry leaves, and cook, stirring occasionally, for 5 minutes or until the onions are soft.

3 Add the spinach, turmeric, chili powder, garam masala, ground coriander, and some salt. Mix well, then add the tomatoes and green bell pepper. Cook, stirring from time to time, for 5 minutes or until the mixture is reduced slightly and thick.

4 Stir in the cream and milk, then bring the mixture to a boil, stirring constantly. Remove the pan from the heat, stir in the fried paneer, and serve.

egg curry

Egg dishes are rarely seen in Indian restaurants in North America and Europe, but they are often made at home in India, especially in rural areas where people tend to keep chickens. Not only do eggs bring protein to meals, they are simple to cook and economical to use. This hard-boiled egg curry is delicious and quick to make.

SERVES 4

6 eggs

3 tablespoons vegetable oil

1 teaspoon mustard seeds

2 garlic cloves, peeled and chopped

2 dried, hot red chili peppers

10 curry leaves

1 onion, peeled and very finely sliced

1 teaspoon hot chili powder

1/2 teaspoon ground coriander

1/2 teaspoon cumin seeds, crushed

1/2 teaspoon ground turmeric

1 teaspoon tomato paste

5 tomatoes, finely diced

1 3/4 cups coconut milk

sea salt

2 tablespoons chopped cilantro for garnish

1 Place the eggs in a large saucepan, cover with water, and slowly bring to a boil. Lower the heat and simmer for 10 minutes. Drain and let cool in a bowl of cold water. Peel away the shells and rinse the eggs to remove any stray pieces of shell, then set aside.

2 Heat the oil in a medium saucepan. Add the mustard seeds and, when they start to pop, add the garlic, dried chilies, and curry leaves, and sauté for 1 minute or until the garlic is golden. Add the onion along with a large pinch of salt and cook, stirring constantly, for 5 minutes or until it is softened.

3 Stir in the chili powder, ground coriander, crushed cumin, and turmeric, then mix in the tomato paste and diced tomatoes. Cook for 5 minutes, stirring constantly, until the sauce is well blended.

4 Lower the heat and pour in the coconut milk, stirring to combine. Gently drop the eggs into the sauce and cook gently for 5 minutes longer or until the eggs are hot and the sauce is thick. Sprinkle with the cilantro before serving.

egg and onion masala

How can I ever forget my favorite canteen meal from university days? The best-selling dish at lunchtime was always paratha with this delicious egg curry. The masala sauce has a lovely hint of coconut and works well as the base for a dish of spicy potatoes. I have also made this curry with green peas instead of eggs, with good results.

SERVES 4

2/3 cup freshly grated coconut

6 extra large eggs

3 tablespoons vegetable oil

pinch of fennel seeds

pinch of fenugreek seeds

2 garlic cloves, peeled and minced

4 medium-hot green chili peppers, slit lengthwise

1-inch piece fresh ginger, peeled and minced

20 curry leaves

3 small onions, peeled and finely sliced

3 tomatoes, chopped

1/2 teaspoon ground turmeric

1/2 teaspoon hot chili powder

sea salt

chopped cilantro for garnish

1 Place the grated coconut and 1/2 cup water in a blender and process until you have a fine paste. Set aside.

2 Place the eggs in a large saucepan, cover with water, and slowly bring to a boil. Lower the heat and simmer for 10 minutes. Drain and let cool in a bowl of cold water. Peel away the shells and rinse the eggs to remove any stray pieces of shell, then set aside.

3 Heat the oil in a large saucepan. Add the fennel and fenugreek seeds and fry until they turn golden, then add the garlic, chilies, ginger, and curry leaves, and sauté for 2–3 minutes. Add the onions and fry for about 5 minutes until they are softened. Add the tomatoes, turmeric, chili powder, and a little salt, and cook for 5 minutes or until the sauce is thick.

4 Lower the heat, then stir in the coconut paste and cook for 5 minutes, stirring occasionally. Halve the hard-boiled eggs lengthwise and add to the pan. Spoon the sauce over them to coat. Warm through gently, then remove the pan from the heat. Serve hot, sprinkled with cilantro. Accompany with rice or appams (pages 158–9).

Indian scrambled eggs

This dish is essentially a thoran, and in India it would be served as part of a substantial meal. However, it is easy enough to make for breakfast or brunch, in which case you need only serve it with bread or rice. The spicing is very simple and light. Using shallots instead of onions helps to keep the flavor mild and sweet.

Illustrated on previous page

SERVES 2

3 extra large eggs
2 tablespoons vegetable oil
1/2 teaspoon mustard seeds
10 curry leaves
4 oz shallots, peeled and finely sliced
1/4 teaspoon ground turmeric
1/4 teaspoon hot chili powder
1 tomato, chopped
sea salt
1 tablespoon chopped cilantro for garnish
  (optional)

1 Break the eggs into a bowl and add a little salt. Whisk with a fork or balloon whisk for 1–2 minutes or until well mixed and bubbles start to form on the surface.

2 Heat the oil in a large frying pan. Add the mustard seeds and, when they start to pop, add the curry leaves and stir-fry for 2 minutes or until fragrant. Add the shallots and cook, stirring, over a low heat for 5 minutes or until softened.

3 Stir in the turmeric and chili powder, then add the tomato and cook gently for 5 minutes. Pour in the beaten eggs. Using a wooden spoon, stir constantly for 3 minutes or so, until they are scrambled to your taste. Remove the pan from the heat and sprinkle with the cilantro, if desired. Serve at once, with plain rice or bread.

spicy eggs with eggplant and spinach

Spicy egg dishes, such as this one, are a favorite with my friend Jamie Oliver, who loves the flavor of chili peppers. The fiery sauce is beautifully balanced by the use of fresh ginger. An ideal partner would be Muslim-style rice with ghee (page 167), or even plain rice, and don't forget to have a cooling raita or some plain yogurt alongside.

SERVES 4–6

6 eggs
4 tablespoons vegetable oil
3 onions, peeled and sliced lengthwise
3 medium-hot green chili peppers, minced
3 garlic cloves, peeled and minced
1-inch piece fresh ginger, peeled and minced
few curry leaves
1 teaspoon tomato paste
1 teaspoon ground coriander
1/2 teaspoon ground turmeric
1/2 teaspoon hot chili powder
1/2 teaspoon garam masala
3 tomatoes, finely sliced
4 oz baby eggplants, quartered
1 cup baby spinach leaves
sea salt

1   Place the eggs in a large saucepan, cover with water, and slowly bring to a boil. Lower the heat and simmer for 10 minutes. Drain and let cool in a bowl of cold water. Peel away the shells and rinse the eggs to remove any stray pieces of shell, then set aside.

2   Heat the oil in a frying pan or wok. Add the onions, chilies, garlic, ginger, and curry leaves, and cook, stirring frequently, for 5 minutes or until the onions are soft. Add the tomato paste, ground coriander, turmeric, chili powder, garam masala, and a little salt. Cook, stirring, for 1 minute.

3   Add the tomatoes, eggplants, and spinach leaves. Cover and cook, stirring from time to time, for 6–7 minutes or until the sauce has blended well with the eggplants and spinach.

4   Add the hard-boiled eggs to the pan and let them heat through gently in the sauce for about 5 minutes before serving.

4 vegetables

shallot and green banana theeyal

This dish is typical of the Nair community, to which I belong, and was a family favorite when I was growing up. It can be made with any chunky vegetable, but shallots are essential. I like to serve theeyal with rice and plain yogurt. You'll find it tastes even better the day after making.

SERVES 4

2 green bananas or plantain, peeled

3 tablespoons vegetable oil

9 oz shallots, peeled and quartered

2 medium-hot green chili peppers, slit lengthwise

1 teaspoon ground turmeric

3 tomatoes, quartered

1/2 teaspoon mustard seeds

10 curry leaves

juice of 1 lime

sea salt

FOR THE SPICED COCONUT LIQUID:

1/2 cup freshly grated coconut

2 tablespoons coriander seeds

3 dried, hot red chili peppers

1 garlic clove, peeled

1 cinnamon stick

1 For the spiced coconut liquid, toast all the ingredients in a large frying pan for 4–5 minutes or until the coconut turns brown. Remove the pan from the heat and let the mixture cool for 5 minutes. Remove the cinnamon stick, then transfer the mixture to a blender. Add 2 cups water and process slowly until evenly blended.

2 Cut the bananas into 1-inch pieces. Heat 2 tablespoons oil in a large saucepan or wok. Add the bananas, shallots, and chilies, and cook for 5 minutes or until the shallots are softened. Add the turmeric, coconut liquid, and salt, and cook on a medium heat, stirring occasionally, for 5 minutes.

3 Mix in the tomatoes and cook over a low heat for 10 minutes or until the shallots are very tender. When the curry is nearly ready, heat the remaining 1 tablespoon oil in a frying pan. Add the mustard seeds and, when they start to pop, add the curry leaves. Pour the contents of the frying pan over the curry and stir through. Add the lime juice and cook over a medium heat for 3 minutes before serving.

vegetable and coconut milk stew

Whenever you eat at a South Indian restaurant, a delicious vegetable and coconut milk stew is almost sure to be on the menu. It is one of the mildest dishes in our repertoire and has plenty of sweet-tasting coconut milk sauce, making it ideal for children, too. Again, you can vary this dish, as we do all the time, with whatever fresh vegetables you have on hand.

Illustrated on previous page

SERVES 4

1 teaspoon ghee or butter
12 shallots, peeled and cut into wedges
1$1/2$ teaspoons all-purpose flour
3 tablespoons tomato paste
$1/2$ teaspoon hot chili powder
$1/2$ teaspoon ground coriander
$1/2$ teaspoon ground turmeric
9 oz pumpkin, peeled and cut into short sticks
7 oz green beans, trimmed
5 oz cauliflower florets
$2/3$ cup green peas
1 cup coconut milk
sea salt

1 Heat the ghee or butter in a large saucepan. Add the shallots and fry, stirring, for 5 minutes or until golden. Remove from the heat and sprinkle in the flour. Stir well and return to a low heat.

2 Slowly add 2 cups water, stirring well to prevent any lumps of flour from forming. Mix in the tomato paste, chili powder, ground coriander, and turmeric, then add the pumpkin, green beans, cauliflower, green peas, and a little salt. Cover and cook, stirring occasionally, for 20 minutes or until all the vegetables are tender.

3 Remove the pan from the heat and slowly pour in the coconut milk. Stir constantly over a low heat for 2 minutes so that it heats through gently and blends with the other ingredients. Serve immediately.

mixed vegetable masala

This is a far cry from the dreary mixed vegetable curry found on most Indian restaurant menus twenty years ago (and sometimes still today). Combining a wide variety of vegetables is the secret to making this dish a treat for vegetarians and meat-eaters alike. You can use any selection of vegetables—try incorporating more unusual varieties such as okra when they are available.

SERVES 4

3 tablespoons vegetable oil

1-inch piece cinnamon stick

3 whole cloves

4–5 green cardamom pods, cracked

pinch of fennel seeds

5 shallots, peeled and minced

4 bell peppers (1 each red, yellow, orange, and green)

4 tomatoes, quartered

3 potatoes, peeled and diced

3 carrots, peeled and diced

$2/3$ cup green peas

2 tablespoons chopped cilantro for garnish

FOR THE SPICE PASTE:

5 tablespoons plain yogurt

1 teaspoon tomato paste

1 teaspoon hot chili powder

$1/2$ teaspoon ground cumin

$1/2$ teaspoon ground turmeric

$1/2$ teaspoon garam masala

1   To make the spice paste, place the yogurt in a small bowl and stir in the tomato paste, chili powder, cumin, turmeric, and garam masala. Set aside.

2   Heat the oil in a large saucepan. Add the cinnamon, cloves, cardamom pods, fennel seeds, and shallots, and cook, stirring occasionally, for 10 minutes or until the shallots are soft and golden. Meanwhile, halve, core, and seed the bell peppers, then cut into dice.

3   Lower the heat under the pan. Add the tomatoes and spicy yogurt paste and mix well. Pour in 2½ cups water and bring the mixture to a boil. Stir in the diced bell peppers, potatoes, carrots, and peas. Cover and cook for 10–15 minutes or until the vegetables are tender. Remove from the heat, sprinkle with the cilantro, and serve.

sweet mango pachadi

Pachadi is a popular feast item among Brahmins in South India, probably because its thick, creamy sauce offers a complete contrast to their usual spicy curries, and it can be made using different fruits. During the mango season we would often make this version for family gatherings.

SERVES 4

7 oz ripe mango

1 oz jaggery or palm sugar (or 3 tablespoons raw brown sugar)

1-inch piece fresh ginger, peeled and finely sliced

1/2 teaspoon ground turmeric

3 tablespoons vegetable oil

1 teaspoon mustard seeds

10 curry leaves

4 dried, hot red chili peppers

sea salt

FOR THE SPICE PASTE:

3/4 cup freshly grated coconut

2 medium-hot green chili peppers

1 teaspoon mustard powder

1   For the spice paste, place all the ingredients in a blender and add 1 cup water. Process slowly to make a coarse paste.

2   Peel the mango and cut the flesh away from the pit, then cut into 1-inch cubes. Place in a large saucepan and cover generously with water. Bring to a boil, then lower the heat and simmer for 5 minutes. Add the jaggery, ginger, turmeric, and a little salt, and simmer for another 5 minutes or until the fruit is thoroughly cooked and the jaggery is well blended.

3   Add the coconut spice paste to the pan and stir to combine with the mango mixture. Lower the heat and cook gently for 5 minutes.

4   Just before it is ready, heat the oil in a small frying pan. Add the mustard seeds and, when they start to pop, add the curry leaves and dried chilies and cook for 1 minute. Pour the contents of the pan over the curry and stir to combine, then serve immediately.

moru

No South Indian meal is complete without a yogurt curry known as moru kachiathu, though you might consider it to be more of a sauce than a curry. A thin, smooth, and vibrantly yellow mixture of yogurt, ginger, and chilies, it seems to enhance the foods it is served with in an almost magical way.

For a light meal, the basic moru can be served simply with cashew and lemon rice (page 166) or appams (pages 158–9). Or, for a more substantial curry, vegetables or fruits can be added, the sourness of the yogurt providing a wonderful contrast to sweet fruits such as mango and plantain.

When making moru, you must remove the pan from the heat before adding the yogurt, otherwise the mixture will curdle. Blend the yogurt in slowly, stirring all the time. Authentically, moru is served warm rather than hot: it is just warmed through gently after the yogurt is added. Each of the following morus serves 4.

▲ **spinach and mango moru curry**
Heat 1 tbsp oil in a pan. Fry 1 tsp mustard seeds and, when they start to pop, add 1 finely sliced small onion, 20 curry leaves, 2 dried, hot red chili peppers, and 1 tsp salt. Cook for 10 minutes. Add 1 tsp grated fresh ginger and 1 medium-hot green chili pepper, slit lengthwise. Cook, stirring, for 1 minute. Mix in 1 tsp turmeric, then off the heat slowly stir in 2 cups plain yogurt. Stir in ¼ cup spinach leaves and 1 thinly sliced small mango. Heat gently, stirring, for 1 minute.

basic moru kachiathu

Heat 1 tbsp oil in a pan and fry 1 tsp mustard seeds until they start to pop. Add 1 finely sliced small onion, 2 dried, hot red chili peppers, 20 curry leaves, and 1 tsp salt. Cook for 10 minutes or until the onion is golden. Add 1 tsp grated fresh ginger and 1 slit medium-hot green chili pepper. Cook, stirring, for 1 minute. Mix in 1 tsp turmeric. Off the heat slowly stir in 2 cups plain yogurt. Reheat gently, stirring.

mixed pepper moru curry

Fry 2 tsp mustard seeds in 4 tbsp oil and, as they start to pop, add 3 minced garlic cloves, 3 dried, hot red chili peppers, 1/4 tsp fenugreek seeds, and 10 curry leaves. Cook for 2 minutes. Add 2 minced onions, 3 slit medium-hot green chili peppers, and 1 tbsp minced ginger; cook for 10 minutes. Stir in 1 chopped tomato, 1 tsp turmeric, and salt, then add 1 1/2 cups mixed bell peppers, cut in strips; cook for 5 minutes. Off the heat, slowly stir in 1 cup plain yogurt. Heat gently for 1 minute, stirring.

▲ okra moru curry

Fry 1 1/2 cups sliced okra in 2 tbsp oil for 5 minutes; drain. Fry 2 tsp mustard seeds in 4 tbsp oil; as they pop add 3 minced garlic cloves, 3 dried, hot red chili peppers, 10 curry leaves, and 1/4 tsp fenugreek seeds. Cook for 2 minutes. Add 2 minced onions, 3 slit medium-hot green chili peppers, and 1 tbsp minced fresh ginger; cook for 10 minutes. Stir in 1 chopped tomato, 1 tsp turmeric, salt, and the okra; cook for 5 minutes. Off the heat, stir in 1 cup plain yogurt. Reheat gently, stirring.

garlic curry

People are always intrigued by this curry and wonder how the strong flavor of garlic is so well tamed by the spicy and tangy tamarind sauce. This is a special recipe given to me by a friend from Karakkudi in Tamil Nadu. It is traditionally eaten with Malabar parathas (page 155).

SERVES 4

3 oz tamarind pulp

3 tablespoons vegetable oil

7 oz garlic cloves, peeled

1 teaspoon fenugreek seeds

2 dried, hot red chili peppers

1/2 teaspoon fennel seeds

10 curry leaves

3 onions, peeled and minced

3 medium-hot green chili peppers, slit lengthwise

1/2 teaspoon ground turmeric

1/2 teaspoon hot chili powder

2 tomatoes, finely diced

1 Place the tamarind pulp in a small bowl and add 4 cups hot water. Break up the tamarind pulp as much as possible, then set aside to soak for 20–30 minutes. Pass through a strainer into another bowl, pressing to extract as much tamarind flavor from the pulp as possible.

2 Heat 1 tablespoon oil in a frying pan. Add 2 oz of the garlic, 1/2 teaspoon fenugreek seeds, and the dried chilies, and fry for 1 minute. Remove with a slotted spoon and drain on paper towels. Transfer the cooked garlic and spices to a blender and process to a fine paste, then set aside.

3 Heat the remaining oil in a large pan. Add the fennel seeds and remaining fenugreek seeds, and sauté for 1 minute or until they are brown. Add the curry leaves, onions, and green chilies. Cook over a medium heat for 5 minutes or until the onions are soft, then add the turmeric and chili powder, followed by the diced tomatoes. Mix well and cook for 5 minutes, stirring frequently.

4 Stir in the remaining garlic cloves, the cooked garlic paste, and the tamarind liquid. Lower the heat and cook gently, stirring frequently, for 15 minutes or until the mixture is thick and the garlic is soft.

green papaya curry

In Indian cooking, fruit is often used in savory dishes as though it were a vegetable, and the distinction between fruit and vegetables is somewhat blurred. To achieve the right flavor and texture in this recipe, make sure that the papaya is green and firm. I love to eat this curry with rice and sweet mango chutney (page 31) for lunch.

SERVES 4

1 firm, unripe papaya, about 9 oz
3 tablespoons vegetable oil
1 teaspoon mustard seeds
pinch of fenugreek seeds
10 curry leaves, plus extra for garnish
3 dried, hot red chili peppers
2/3 cup minced shallots
1-inch piece fresh ginger, peeled and
* finely sliced*
4 medium-hot green chili peppers, slit lengthwise
1 cup coconut milk
sea salt

1 Peel and chop the papaya and place in a large saucepan. Cover generously with water and add a little salt. Bring to a boil, then lower the heat and simmer for 15 minutes or until the papaya is tender. Drain and set aside.

2 Heat the oil in a large saucepan or wok. Add the mustard seeds and, when they start to pop, add the fenugreek seeds. Sauté for 1 minute or until the seeds just turn golden. Add the curry leaves, dried chilies, and shallots, and cook for 5 minutes or until the shallots are lightly golden.

3 Add the ginger, green chilies, and a pinch of salt. Stir well, then add the cooked papaya and stir again. Turn the heat right down and slowly add the coconut milk. Remove the pan from the heat and stir the curry constantly for 2 minutes so that the coconut milk heats through gently. Garnish with fresh curry leaves to serve.

zucchini curry

Although the zucchini is not an Indian vegetable, I was keen to try cooking it with traditional Keralan spices. The refreshing taste of tomatoes with crushed fennel makes this very different from a lot of other curries we offer, and the method of grinding them to a rough paste before cooking is a little unusual, too.

SERVES 4

3 tomatoes
2 garlic cloves, peeled
pinch of fennel seeds
3 tablespoons vegetable oil
1 cup chopped shallots or onion
2 cups sliced zucchini
$1/2$ teaspoon ground turmeric
1 teaspoon hot chili powder
$1^1/4$ cups coconut milk

1   Put the tomatoes, garlic cloves, and fennel seeds in a blender and process to make a rough paste. Set aside.

2   Heat the oil in a large saucepan, karahi, or wok. Add the shallots and cook for 5 minutes or until soft. Add the zucchini, turmeric, and chili powder, and stir-fry for 5 minutes or until the zucchini are tender but still crunchy.

3   Lower the heat and add the freshly ground tomato paste. Cook, stirring well, for 1 minute, then mix in the coconut milk. Bring to a boil, stirring, then lower the heat and simmer for 5 minutes. Serve hot, with rice or bread.

green pea and pepper curry

I have fond memories of the Cotton Hill canteen in Trivandrum, which I used to visit frequently during my university days. The green pea curry, made with a tomato and onion masala and an abundant dose of cracked black pepper, was so tasty that my mouth begins to water at the very thought of it. You should serve this as they used to—with a Malabar paratha (page 155).

SERVES 4

3 tablespoons vegetable oil

1-inch piece fresh ginger, peeled and
  grated

4 shallots, peeled and minced

2 medium-hot green chili peppers, slit lengthwise

1 teaspoon ground coriander

1 teaspoon garam masala

1/2 teaspoon ground turmeric

1/2 teaspoon hot chili powder

4 tomatoes, finely sliced

2 cups green peas

1 red bell pepper, cored, seeded, and chopped

1 teaspoon cracked black pepper

sea salt

2 tablespoons minced cilantro for garnish
  (optional)

1 Heat the oil in a large frying pan, karahi, or wok. Add the grated ginger and sauté for a few seconds, then add the shallots and cook for 5 minutes or until they are soft.

2 Add the chilies, ground coriander, garam masala, turmeric, and chili powder. Stir briefly, then add the sliced tomatoes and a little salt. Pour in 1/2 cup water and mix well, then cover and cook for 5 minutes until the sauce is thick.

3 Lower the heat and add the peas and red bell pepper. Cook gently for 10 minutes or until the vegetables are tender. Stir in the cracked black pepper, then sprinkle with the cilantro, if desired. Serve hot, with parathas.

cauliflower curry

Cauliflower is very popular in North India, and the most typical dish, *aloo gobi*, is found on most restaurant menus. This fresh-tasting curry is best eaten with Malabar parathas (page 155) or cashew and lemon rice (page 166).

SERVES 4

3 tablespoons vegetable oil
1 teaspoon fennel seeds
1 large onion, peeled and minced
1/2 teaspoon ground turmeric
1/2 teaspoon hot chili powder
1/4 cup tomato paste
9 oz cauliflower florets
1 1/4 cups cubed green bell pepper
4 tomatoes, quartered
2 1/2 cups milk
small bunch of cilantro, minced
sea salt

1 Heat the oil in a medium saucepan. Add the fennel seeds and cook, stirring constantly, for 1 minute or until golden brown. Add the onion and cook for 10 minutes, stirring frequently, until golden.

2 Add the turmeric and chili powder, and stir-fry for 2 minutes, then stir in the tomato paste. Add the cauliflower florets, green bell pepper, tomatoes, milk, 1 cup water, and some salt. Cook over a medium heat for 5–8 minutes, stirring constantly to prevent the milk from splitting.

3 When the vegetables are tender, sprinkle with the cilantro, toss to mix, and serve hot.

broccoli with panch phoron

Every state in India has its own special spice blend that becomes a feature of its cooking and brings a distinctive flavor to the characteristic dishes of the region. Bengal in the northeast is known for its homemade spice powder called panch phoron, which combines equal quantities of five strongly flavored spices. It is primarily used in vegetarian dishes to enhance flavor and create a pure Bengali aroma. It's easy to make a batch yourself, to keep and use as required.

SERVES 4

3 tablespoons vegetable oil

1 large onion, peeled and sliced

1-inch piece fresh ginger, peeled and
   shredded

2 dried, hot red chili peppers, chopped

$1/2$ teaspoon ground turmeric

1 cup finely chopped broccoli

$1^2/_3$ cups finely sliced white or green cabbage

1 tablespoon ghee

sea salt

FOR THE SPICE POWDER:

2 teaspoons cumin seeds

2 teaspoons fennel seeds

2 teaspoons fenugreek seeds

2 teaspoons mustard seeds

2 teaspoons kalonji (nigella) seeds

1 To make the spice powder, put all the ingredients in a small spice mill and grind to a fine powder. Store in an airtight container.

2 Heat the oil in a large saucepan, karahi, or wok. Add the onion and ginger, and cook for about 10 minutes or until golden. Add the chilies and turmeric and stir well, then add the broccoli, cabbage, and a little salt. Sprinkle a few tablespoons of water over the vegetable mixture and cover with a lid. Lower the heat and cook for 10 minutes or until the vegetables are tender.

3 Just before the vegetables are cooked, melt the ghee in a small frying pan. Add 1 teaspoon of the panch phoron spice powder. Stir once, then quickly pour the contents of the frying pan over the broccoli mixture. Mix well and serve, with chapattis (page 154) or other Indian bread.

pumpkin curry

We grow a variety of pumpkins in South India, and for each type there is a particular recipe that best highlights its unique texture and flavor. This recipe is a traditional and colorful feast dish, and the use of roasted coconut really makes it stand out from other dishes on the table. Serve it with a moru curry (page 88) and plain rice.

SERVES 4

1 small pumpkin or butternut squash, about 1 lb
1 teaspoon ground turmeric
1 teaspoon hot chili powder
2 cups freshly grated coconut
1/2 teaspoon cumin seeds

3 tablespoons vegetable oil
1 teaspoon mustard seeds
few curry leaves
2 dried, hot red chili peppers
sea salt

1 Peel, seed, and cube the pumpkin, then place in a saucepan with the turmeric, chili powder, a little salt, and 2 1/2 cups water. Bring to a boil, then simmer for 5 minutes or until well cooked.

2 Meanwhile, finely grind half of the coconut with the cumin seeds in a spice mill. Stir into the pumpkin mixture and cook for 2 minutes longer, stirring frequently. Remove from the heat.

3 Heat the oil in a frying pan. Add the mustard seeds and, as they start to pop, add the curry leaves, dried chilies, and remaining coconut. Cook for about 4 minutes until the coconut is toasted. Tip the coconut mixture over the pumpkin curry, stir, and serve.

sweet potato curry

A curry made from sweet potato is something unusual. Care must be taken to balance the spices with the sweetness of the vegetable, so follow the quantities precisely.

SERVES 4

14 oz sweet potatoes, peeled and diced
3 medium-hot green chili peppers
1-inch piece fresh ginger, peeled and
   thinly sliced

1 cup coconut milk
10 curry leaves
sea salt

1 Put the sweet potatoes in a large saucepan with the chilies and ginger. Add just enough water to cover and a pinch of salt. Bring to a boil, then simmer, stirring occasionally, for 10 minutes or until the potatoes are tender.

2 Lower the heat and stir in the coconut milk and curry leaves. Simmer gently, stirring, for a few minutes to heat through, then serve.

5 fish and shellfish

marinated sardines

Fish dishes are hugely popular in India's coastal states and this recipe is typical of Cochin and other backwater areas, where it is eaten for lunch. You only have to walk around the town to savor its tempting aroma, because so many people will be cooking it. Although sardines work particularly well cooked in this way, you can use other oily fish, too.

SERVES 2–3

1 lb sardines, cleaned

4 tablespoons vegetable oil

FOR THE SPICE PASTE:

2 tablespoons lemon juice

1-inch piece fresh ginger, peeled and
  chopped

4 garlic cloves, peeled and crushed

1 teaspoon hot chili powder

large pinch of ground turmeric

sea salt

FOR SERVING:

lime wedges

1 First make the spice paste: Grind the lemon juice, ginger, garlic, chili powder, turmeric, and a little salt together to a fine paste, using a pestle and mortar or a small blender.

2 Using a sharp knife, slash the sardines diagonally on both sides to allow the flavorings to permeate the flesh. Lay them side by side in a non-metallic dish, rub the spice paste all over, and set aside to marinate for 10 minutes.

3 Heat the oil in a large frying pan. Cook the sardines in batches if necessary: Place in a single layer in the pan and fry over a low heat for about 2–3 minutes on each side until brown and crisp. Serve hot, with lime wedges.

tuna and potato cakes

Tuna cakes are often sold as a snack in Indian bakeries. Serve these with a fresh chutney, or garlic and chili pickle (page 27). Shaped into smaller patties, they make a good party snack.

MAKES 6–8

10 oz tuna steaks, cubed

2 cups peeled and cubed potato

1/2 teaspoon ground turmeric, plus a pinch

2 tablespoons vegetable oil

1 teaspoon mustard seeds

10 curry leaves

1-inch piece fresh ginger, peeled and chopped

1 medium-hot green chili pepper, chopped

2 onions, peeled and chopped

1/2 teaspoon hot chili powder

1 teaspoon garam masala

1 1/4 cups cornstarch

about 1 cup fine, dry bread crumbs

vegetable oil for deep-frying

sea salt

1 Put the tuna, potato cubes, 1/2 teaspoon turmeric, and a little salt in a saucepan. Add enough water just to cover and simmer until the potato is just cooked, about 15 minutes. Drain and transfer to a bowl.

2 Heat 2 tablespoons oil in a large frying pan. Add the mustard seeds and, as they start to pop, add the curry leaves, ginger, chili, and onions. Sauté for 5 minutes or until the onions are soft. Add the chili powder, garam masala, and pinch of turmeric. Cook gently for 2 minutes, stirring. Add to the tuna and potato, and mash the mixture. Leave until cool enough to handle.

3 Divide the tuna mixture into six to eight equal portions. Using wet hands, form into teardrop-shaped cakes. Blend the cornstarch with 1 cup water. Spread the bread crumbs on a baking sheet. Heat the oil for deep-frying in a suitable pan to 350°–375°F.

4 Dip each cake into the cornstarch liquid, then coat with the bread crumbs, pressing them on gently. Deep-fry in batches for 3–5 minutes until golden, turning frequently. Drain on paper towels and serve.

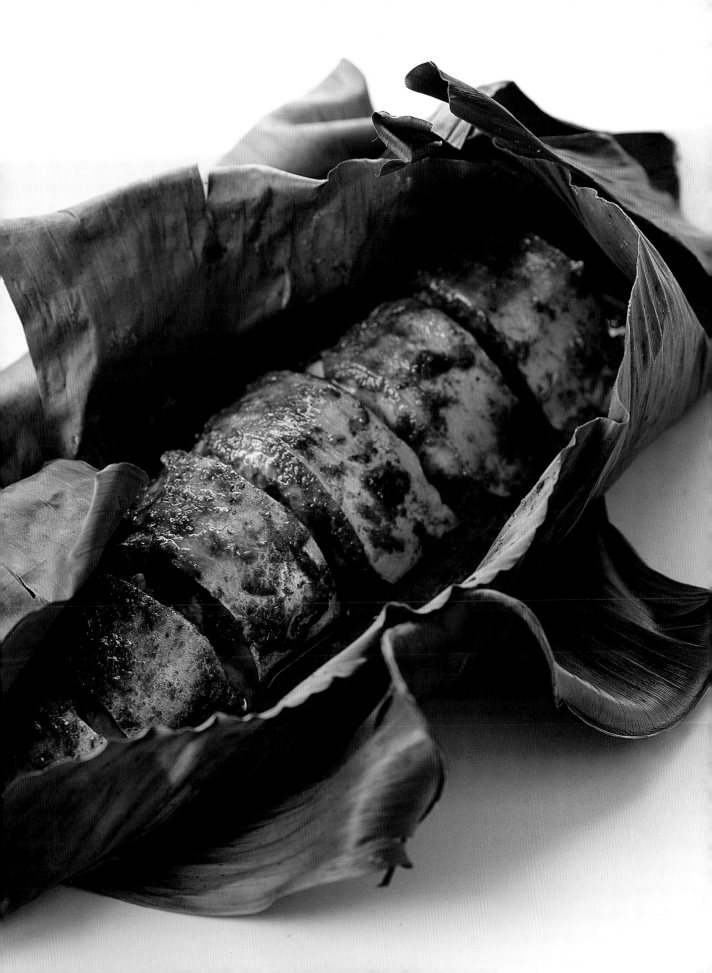

fish steamed in banana leaves

This dish is renowned in Kerala, where steamed fish, known as *meen elayil pollichathu*, are popular. Steaming allows you to enjoy the full flavor of the fish, and banana leaves add a special essence to the final dish. If you cannot find banana leaves, foil is a good alternative.

Illustrated on previous page

SERVES 2–4

2 mackerel, each about 12 oz, cleaned and
  cut across into 1-inch slices
1 large banana leaf

FOR THE SPICE PASTE:
2 cups cilantro leaves, chopped
1 onion, peeled and chopped
3 garlic cloves, peeled and chopped
$^1/_2$-inch piece fresh ginger, peeled and
  chopped
1 medium-hot green chili pepper, chopped
$^1/_2$ teaspoon ground black pepper
2 tablespoons lime juice
sea salt

1 To make the spice paste, place the chopped cilantro, onion, garlic, ginger, chili, black pepper, and lime juice in a blender. Add a little salt and process to a smooth paste.

2 Transfer the spice paste to a large bowl. Add the fish pieces and rub the paste carefully into the flesh. Set aside to marinate for 10 minutes.

3 Position a large steamer over a pan of water and bring to a boil. Dip the banana leaf briefly in a bowl of hot water to soften and make it pliable, then shake gently to remove excess water. Spread it out on a work surface.

4 Place the fish on the banana leaf, re-assembling it if you like, and spread the excess spice paste on top of the fish. Carefully wrap the leaf around the fish to make a parcel. Secure with string, strips of banana leaf, or small skewers. Place the parcel in the steamer and cook for 5–6 minutes.

5 To serve, lift the banana-wrapped fish onto a hot platter. Unwrap the parcel at the table so that everyone can savor the aroma.

sole in tamarind sauce

This spicy, red-colored dish has an unforgettable and distinctive flavor, thanks to the use of tamarind. In India, it would be cooked in a terracotta pot over a slow fire. Although I'm using sole here, any similar white flatfish can be substituted.

SERVES 6

2oz tamarind pulp

2 tablespoons vegetable oil

1 teaspoon mustard seeds

10 curry leaves

pinch of fenugreek seeds

2 onions, peeled and chopped

$\frac{1}{4}$ teaspoon ground turmeric

$\frac{1}{2}$ teaspoon hot chili powder

1 teaspoon ground coriander

3 tomatoes, chopped

1 teaspoon tomato paste

1$\frac{1}{4}$ lb sole or flounder fillets

sea salt

1 Place the tamarind pulp in a small heatproof bowl and break it up as much as possible. Add $\frac{1}{2}$ cup hot water and set aside to soak for 20 minutes. Press the mixture through a strainer into a bowl and set aside, discarding the residue in the strainer.

2 Meanwhile, heat the oil in a large saucepan, karahi, or wok. Add the mustard seeds and, when they start to pop, add the curry leaves and fenugreek seeds. Sauté for 1–2 minutes or until the fenugreek seeds turn brown. Stir in the onions and cook over a medium heat, stirring occasionally, for 10 minutes or until they are golden.

3 Add the turmeric, chili powder, and ground coriander. Mix well, then add the chopped tomatoes, tomato paste, and a little salt. Cook for 2 minutes longer. Pour in the tamarind liquid and 1 cup water. Bring the mixture to a boil and simmer for 10–12 minutes, stirring occasionally, until the sauce thickens.

4 Cut the fish fillets into 1-inch pieces and carefully mix into the sauce. Lower the heat and cook gently for 4–5 minutes or until the fish is just cooked through. Remove the pan from the heat and serve immediately.

sole with coconut

The use of coconut milk in fish curries is typical of the inland areas of Kerala. Its smooth, creamy taste provides a soothing quality that appeals to those who prefer mild curries, and it certainly makes the dish look appetizing. Other white fish can be used instead of sole, if you prefer.

SERVES 6

2 tablespoons vegetable oil

1¼ cups chopped shallots

10 curry leaves

1¼ lb sole or flounder fillets

FOR THE SPICE PASTE:

1 cup freshly grated coconut

1 teaspoon ground coriander

½ teaspoon hot chili powder

large pinch of ground turmeric

1 To make the spice paste, place the coconut, ground coriander, chili powder, and turmeric in a blender. Pour in 1 cup water and process for 2–3 minutes to a smooth paste. Set aside.

2 Heat the oil in a large frying pan, karahi, or wok. Add the shallots and curry leaves, and cook over a medium-low heat for 5 minutes or until the shallots are soft. Stir in the coconut spice paste along with ¼ cup water and bring the mixture to a boil. Cook for about 5 minutes, stirring occasionally, until the sauce thickens.

3 Cut the fish fillets into 1-inch pieces, add to the sauce, and mix in carefully. Cook gently for 4–5 minutes or until the fish is cooked through. Remove the pan from the heat and serve immediately.

salmon curry

This fish curry is popular in toddy shops (local village bars) across India, and so famously delicious that even teetotallers visit regularly to enjoy it. Here I am using salmon, but of course in India it would be prepared with the local catch. Accompany with rice or potatoes.

SERVES 4–6

1 tablespoon tamarind pulp

2 tablespoons vegetable oil

1/2 teaspoon mustard seeds

10 curry leaves

pinch of fenugreek seeds

1 large onion, peeled and chopped

1/2 teaspoon ground turmeric

1/2 teaspoon hot chili powder

1 teaspoon ground coriander

2 tomatoes, chopped

1 lb salmon fillet, cubed

1 cup coconut milk

sea salt

1 Place the tamarind pulp in a small heatproof bowl and cover with 3 tablespoons hot water. Use a teaspoon to break up the tamarind as much as possible, then set aside to soften for 15–20 minutes. Push the mixture through a strainer to extract 3 tablespoons of tamarind-flavored liquid; discard any seeds and fibers.

2 Meanwhile, heat the oil in a large saucepan, karahi, or wok. Add the mustard seeds and, when they start to pop, add the curry leaves and fenugreek seeds. Fry for 1 minute or until golden. Add the onion and cook over a medium-low heat for 10 minutes, stirring occasionally, until golden.

3 Add the turmeric, chili powder, and ground coriander, and cook for a further minute. Add the tomatoes and a little salt, and cook for 2 minutes, stirring constantly. Pour in the tamarind liquid and 1 1/4 cups water and slowly bring to a boil.

4 Meanwhile, cut the salmon into 1 1/2-inch pieces. Lower the heat under the pan, add the fish pieces, and simmer gently for 5–6 minutes or until the salmon is just cooked through.

5 Turn the heat as low as possible and pour in the coconut milk. Simmer very gently for 2 minutes, then remove the pan from the heat and serve immediately.

fried fish Indian-style

Here is India's spicy take on fish and chips. Fried fish in batter is often made at home on the subcontinent, but more importantly, it's a favorite snack sold in India's popular *thattukada,* or street refreshment places.

The secret of successful deep-frying is to make sure that the oil is at the correct temperature before the batter-coated fish is added. The oil should register 350°–375°F on a thermometer, or you can test by adding a cube of bread—this should brown in 30 seconds. It is also important that the pan is not overcrowded, because this will lower the temperature of the oil. Add the coated pieces of fish one or two at a time.

In India, fried batter-coated fish is generally eaten plain, but I've suggested suitable chutneys to accompany, if you prefer. These batter recipes are enough to coat 1 lb fish or seafood, which will serve 4. Experiment with different fish and shellfish, according to availability.

▲ **spiced batter**

In a blender, mix ¾ cup chick pea flour with ½ cup rice flour, 4 tbsp chopped cilantro, 1 chopped medium-hot green chili pepper, 1 tsp hot chili powder, ½ tsp garam masala, a pinch of turmeric, and a little salt. Slowly blend in about 1 cup water to make a smooth batter. Cut 1 lb fish fillets into strips. Dip in the batter, then deep-fry in hot oil for 1 minute until golden. Serve with sweet mango chutney (page 31).

hot pepper batter

Mix 1⅓ cups all-purpose flour, ½ tsp baking powder, 1 tsp crushed black pepper, pinch of salt, 1 tsp hot chili powder, and ¼ tsp ground turmeric in a bowl. Whisk 4 eggs with 6 tbsp milk, then pour into the flour mixture and gradually mix to a smooth, thick batter. Let rest for 20 minutes. Cut 1 lb fish fillets into strips, dip in the batter, and deep-fry in hot oil for 1 minute until golden. Serve plain or with a chutney.

▲ spiced coconut milk batter

Put 1¼ cups cornstarch in a bowl with 3 minced garlic cloves, a 1-inch piece fresh ginger, minced, 10 chopped curry leaves, 1 tsp hot chili powder, ¼ tsp turmeric, and a little salt. Make a well in the center and add 1 beaten egg, then ½ cup coconut milk. Mix to a smooth, thick batter. Cut 1 lb fish fillets into strips, dip in the batter, and deep-fry in hot oil for 1 minute until golden. Serve plain or with sweet mango chutney (page 31).

▲ spinach and curry leaf batter

In a blender, mix ¾ cup chick pea flour with ½ cup rice flour, ½ cup minced spinach leaves, 20 minced curry leaves, 1 chopped medium-hot green chili pepper, 1 tsp hot chili powder, ½ tsp garam masala, a pinch of turmeric, and a little salt. Slowly blend in 1 cup water to make a smooth batter. Peel 1 lb raw tiger shrimp, leaving the tails on. Dip into the batter, then deep-fry in the hot oil for 1–2 minutes until crisp and golden. Serve with coconut chutney (page 30).

shrimp stir-fry

Rahul Dravid, one of India's most famous cricketers, came to our restaurant in London last year and asked us to make him a crunchy shrimp dish with plenty of curry leaves and onions. He told me how his mother always made a dish like this for him during his occasional visits back home. Our attempt couldn't have been too bad—Rahul liked it so much he returned four times. It is easy to make at home, and full of crunchy textures and fresh flavors.

SERVES 4

14 oz medium or large shrimp (preferably raw),
  peeled and deveined
vegetable oil for deep-frying
2 tablespoons vegetable oil
¹/₂ teaspoon mustard seeds
10 curry leaves
1 cup sliced shallots
¹/₂ teaspoon ground turmeric
¹/₂ teaspoon hot chili powder
1 medium-hot green chili pepper, slit lengthwise
1 tablespoon lemon juice
¹/₂ teaspoon ground black pepper
sea salt

1 Cut the shrimp into ¹/₂-inch pieces. Heat the oil for deep-frying in a large, heavy-based saucepan, karahi, or wok to 350°–375°F, or until a cube of bread browns in 30 seconds. Add the shrimp and deep-fry until lightly golden—45 seconds for cooked shrimp; 1¹/₂ minutes for raw. Remove with a slotted spoon and set aside to drain on paper towels.

2 Heat 2 tablespoons oil in a large frying pan, karahi, or wok. Add the mustard seeds and, when they start to pop, add the curry leaves and shallots. Cook, stirring, for 5 minutes or until the shallots are soft. Stir in the turmeric, chili powder, green chili pepper, and some salt. Cook, stirring, for 2 minutes.

3 Add the shrimp and stir-fry over a medium-low heat for 5 minutes. Pour in the lemon juice, then stir in the black pepper. Rremove the pan from the heat and serve immediately.

shrimp with toasted coconut sauce

We are following in the footsteps of an old Hindu dish with this recipe. The toasted coconut spice paste is often used in vegetable dishes, too. We serve this popular dish with adipoli parathas (page 156); add a side dish of thoran (pages 42–3) and you will have an excellent meal.

SERVES 4–6

3 tablespoons vegetable oil

1/2 teaspoon mustard seeds

10 curry leaves

1 large onion, peeled and chopped

1/2 teaspoon ground turmeric

1/2 teaspoon hot chili powder

2 tomatoes, quartered

1 lb raw medium or large shrimp, peeled and deveined

1/4 cup coconut milk

2 tablespoons lime juice

sea salt

FOR THE SPICE PASTE:

2 tablespoons coriander seeds

1 cup freshly grated coconut

10 curry leaves

1 dried, hot red chili pepper

1   To make the spice paste, place all the ingredients in a frying pan and toast over a medium-low heat, stirring constantly, for 5 minutes or until the coconut turns brown. Set aside to cool.

2   Transfer the toasted coconut mixture to a blender or food processor and process, gradually adding 1¼ cups water to make a thin, smooth paste. Set aside.

3   Heat the oil in a large saucepan, karahi, or wok. Add the mustard seeds and, when they start to pop, add the curry leaves and onion. Cook for 10 minutes, stirring occasionally, until the onion is light golden. Add the turmeric, chili powder, tomatoes, and a little salt, and cook, stirring, for 2 minutes.

4   Pour in the coconut paste, then increase the heat and bring the mixture to a boil. Add the shrimp and simmer for 5 minutes or until they turn pink and are cooked. Lower the heat, stir in the coconut milk, and simmer gently for 2 minutes. Remove the pan from the heat, stir in the lime juice, and serve.

shrimp and mango curry

In India, shrimp are very expensive and considered a luxury food. Consequently, a shrimp curry like this is something enjoyed only on special occasions. Serve this light, mild dish with a rice dish or appams (pages 158–9).

SERVES 4–6

2 tablespoons vegetable oil

$1/2$ teaspoon mustard seeds

10 curry leaves

1-inch piece fresh ginger, peeled and
  cut into julienne strips

2 medium-hot green chili peppers, slit lengthwise

2 large onions, peeled and sliced

1 unripened mango, peeled, pitted, and cubed

$1/2$ teaspoon ground turmeric

$1^3/_4$ cups coconut milk

1 lb raw tiger or jumbo shrimp, peeled
  (tails left on) and deveined

sea salt

1 Heat the oil in a large frying pan, karahi, or wok. Add the mustard seeds and, when they start to pop, add the curry leaves, ginger, chilies, and onions. Cook over a medium-low heat for 10 minutes, stirring occasionally, until the onions are golden.

2 Add the mango, turmeric, and a little salt, and mix well for 1 minute, then pour in the coconut milk and 1 cup water. Bring the mixture to a boil, stirring constantly.

3 Add the shrimp to the pan and cook, stirring, for 5–6 minutes or until they turn pink and are cooked. Serve immediately, with rice or appams.

shrimp and tomato curry

This authentic Keralan recipe originates from Koyilandi near Calicut in the north of the state. It has a thick consistency, making it a good alternative to the more usual sauced dishes. For a complete meal, serve it with adipoli parathas (page 156) and a dish of spicy new potatoes with spinach (page 53). Alternatively, serve the curry on lightly toasted poppadoms.

SERVES 4–6

3 tablespoons vegetable oil
pinch of cumin seeds
10 curry leaves
3 onions, peeled and sliced
1/2 teaspoon ground turmeric
1 teaspoon hot chili powder
1 teaspoon tomato paste
4 tomatoes, sliced
1 lb raw tiger or jumbo shrimp, peeled
  (tails left on) and deveined
sea salt
chopped cilantro for garnish

1 Heat the oil in a large frying pan, karahi, or wok. Add the cumin seeds, curry leaves, and onions, and cook over a medium-low heat for 10 minutes, stirring occasionally, until the onions are golden.

2 Add the turmeric, chili powder, tomato paste, tomatoes, and a little salt. Cook for 5 minutes, stirring constantly.

3 Add the shrimp and cook for 5–6 minutes longer or until they turn pink and are cooked through. Serve sprinkled with chopped cilantro.

pepper-fried crab

If you want to eat crab, this is the way to do it: make a mess and thoroughly enjoy it. Some people complain about the difficulty of extracting the meat from the shell, but it is well worth the effort. People tell me this is the best crab dish they have ever tasted.

SERVES 2–4

1 cooked crab, about 1 lb, cleaned
2 tablespoons ghee
1/2-inch piece fresh ginger, peeled and crushed
2 garlic cloves, peeled and crushed
10 curry leaves

1 large red onion, peeled and sliced
1/2 teaspoon ground turmeric
1 medium-hot green chili pepper, finely sliced
2 tomatoes, cut into wedges
3 tablespoons lemon juice
1 teaspoon ground black pepper
sea salt

1   Using a strong knife, halve or quarter the crab. Make sure that the small stomach sac behind the mouth and the inedible, feathery gray gills ("dead man's fingers") are removed.

2   Heat the ghee in a large frying pan, karahi, or wok. Add the ginger, garlic, curry leaves, and red onion, and stir-fry over a medium-low heat for 3 minutes.

3   Add the turmeric, chopped chili, tomato wedges, and some salt to the pan and continue stir-frying for 2 minutes.

4   Increase the heat slightly, then add the crab pieces and stir-fry for 2 minutes. Lower the heat, add the lemon juice and black pepper, and cook gently for 3 minutes longer. Serve immediately.

crab thoran

Fresh coconut gives this simple recipe a lovely light texture. It is a dry dish that can be eaten on its own or as a side dish. Here it is made with crabmeat, but it also works well with shrimp.

SERVES 4

2 tablespoons vegetable oil

1/2 teaspoon mustard seeds

10 curry leaves

3 garlic cloves, peeled and chopped

1-inch piece fresh ginger, peeled and minced

2 large onions, peeled and chopped

1 1/2 cups freshly grated coconut

1/2 teaspoon ground turmeric

1/2 teaspoon hot chili powder

1/2 teaspoon ground black pepper

14 oz cooked white crabmeat

sea salt

1 Heat the oil in a large frying pan, karahi, or wok. Add the mustard seeds and, when they start to pop, add the curry leaves, garlic, ginger, and onions. Cook over a medium-low heat, stirring occasionally, for 5 minutes or until the onions are soft.

2 Add the grated coconut, turmeric, chili powder, black pepper, and a little salt, and stir-fry for 2 minutes. Increase the heat slightly, then add the crabmeat and continue stir-frying for 4–5 minutes. Serve at once.

curried mussels

When I visited Beppoor Port in the north of Kerala during a spice trail trip last year, we came across mussel dishes in almost every restaurant. This is thanks to Arabic trade in the area centuries ago, when Kerala was a regular stop on the way to Sri Lanka. Beppoor Port boasts many mussel dishes including spicy stir-fries, steamed rice dishes, and mussels in coconut sauce. My guests found this one most simple and tasty.

SERVES 2–4

1 lb fresh mussels
2 tablespoons vegetable oil
1/2 teaspoon cumin seeds
1 bay leaf
5 garlic cloves, peeled and minced
2 onions, peeled and minced
1/2 teaspoon ground turmeric, plus a large pinch
2 tomatoes, finely diced
2 tablespoons lime juice
2 tablespoons chopped cilantro
sea salt

1 Clean the mussels by scrubbing the shells under cold running water and removing any beards that are attached to them. Discard any with cracked or broken shells, or any that refuse to close when tapped sharply with a knife. Set the prepared mussels aside.

2 Heat the oil in a large frying pan. Add the cumin seeds, bay leaf, garlic, and onions, and fry for about 5 minutes until the onions are soft. Add 1/2 teaspoon turmeric, a pinch of salt, and the tomatoes. Cook over a low heat, stirring well, for 3 minutes.

3 Meanwhile, put the mussels in a large saucepan with a large pinch of turmeric and a little salt. Add cold water to cover and bring to a boil. Simmer for 2–3 minutes or until the mussels have steamed opened. Discard any that do not open.

4 Quickly drain the mussels, reserving the cooking liquid. Add the mussels to the onion mixture and cook, stirring, for 2 minutes. If you would like the sauce to be thinner, add some of the reserved mussel cooking water. Add the lime juice and chopped cilantro. Remove from the heat and serve immediately.

6 poultry and meat

marinated chicken with hot pepper sauce

The Andhra Pradesh region is well known for its fiery dishes that use a variety of chili peppers. People there believe that chili was the first thing grown in the world and that it should be the main ingredient of any dish, so you can imagine how hot the food can get! Not everyone can handle chilies in the same way, however, and, after a point, adding more chili to a dish does not necessarily make it taste better in my opinion. So here is a moderately fiery version.

SERVES 4

4 chicken portions (quarters or breast halves)

4 garlic cloves, peeled and chopped

1-inch piece fresh ginger, peeled and
   sliced

3 tablespoons vegetable oil

10 curry leaves

2 onions, peeled and minced

2 teaspoons ground coriander

$1/2$ teaspoon hot chili powder

$1/2$ teaspoon ground turmeric

2 tomatoes, chopped

1 teaspoon ground black pepper

FOR THE SPICE PASTE:

1 teaspoon garam masala

$1/2$ teaspoon ground turmeric

sea salt

1 To make the spice paste, mix the garam masala, turmeric, and a little salt with about 2 tablespoons water in a small bowl. Place the chicken pieces in a shallow, non-metallic dish and spread the paste all over them. Set aside to marinate for 10 minutes.

2 Meanwhile, using a mortar and pestle or small spice mill, grind the garlic and ginger together to make a paste. Set aside.

3 Heat the oil in a saucepan, karahi, or wok. Add the curry leaves and onions, and fry for 2 minutes, then add the garlic-ginger paste and cook, stirring occasionally, for 5 minutes or until the onions are soft. Add the ground coriander, chili powder, and turmeric, and stir well, then add the tomatoes and a little salt. Cook gently for 1–2 minutes.

4 Lay the marinated chicken pieces in the pan, spooning some of the onion mixture over the top. Pour in $2^{1}/2$ cups water and bring to a simmer. Cook for 20–25 minutes or until the chicken is cooked through. Stir in the black pepper and cook for 2 minutes longer, then serve hot.

chicken with roasted coconut

There is nothing quite like the wonderful aroma of freshly roasted coconut. The ingredients in this recipe are beautifully balanced and the resulting dish has a lovely color and natural creamy coconut flavor.

SERVES 4

1 lb skinless, boneless chicken thighs
3 tablespoons vegetable oil
1/2 teaspoon mustard seeds
10 curry leaves
2 onions, peeled and finely sliced
2 tomatoes, chopped
1/2 teaspoon ground turmeric
sea salt

FOR THE SPICE PASTE:

1 tablespoon vegetable oil
1 cup freshly grated coconut
2 bay leaves
1 cinnamon stick
1/2 teaspoon ground black pepper
2 whole cloves
1 teaspoon ground coriander
1/2 teaspoon hot chili powder

1 To make the spice paste, heat the oil in a frying pan. Add the coconut, bay leaves, cinnamon stick, black pepper, and cloves, and toast, stirring constantly, for 3–5 minutes or until the coconut is golden.

2 Remove from the heat and stir in the ground coriander and chili powder. Discard the cinnamon stick. Tip into a blender, pour in 1³⁄4 cups water, and process for 3–5 minutes to a fine paste. Set aside.

3 Cut the chicken into thick strips and set aside. Heat 3 tablespoons oil in a large saucepan, karahi, or wok. Add the mustard seeds and, when they start to pop, add the curry leaves and onions. Cook, stirring frequently, for 5 minutes or until the onions are soft.

4 Add the tomatoes, turmeric, and a little salt, and stir-fry for 2 minutes. Add the chicken, coconut paste, and 2¹⁄2 cups water, and bring to a simmer. Cook gently for 15–20 minutes or until the chicken is cooked through. Serve hot.

home-style chicken

Known as *kozhy curry*, this dish is often made at home in India. It is quick and simple, and uses ingredients that are easy to find—an ideal recipe for those who have little time to cook. Boneless chicken thighs are convenient, but using chicken on the bone will give the sauce a richer flavor. *Illustrated on previous page*

SERVES 4

3 tablespoons vegetable oil
1-inch piece cinnamon stick
2 bay leaves
3 whole cloves
2 onions, peeled and chopped
10 curry leaves
1 tablespoon ground coriander
1 teaspoon garam masala
1/2 teaspoon ground turmeric
1/2 teaspoon hot chili powder
2 tomatoes, finely diced
1 lb skinless, boneless chicken thighs, cubed,
* or 13/4 lb chicken pieces with bone*
sea salt
2 tablespoons chopped cilantro for garnish

1 Heat the oil in a large saucepan or heavy casserole. Add the cinnamon stick, bay leaves, and cloves, and cook for 1–2 minutes or until fragrant. Add the onions and curry leaves, and cook, stirring occasionally, for 5 minutes or until the onions are soft.

2 Stir in the ground coriander, garam masala, turmeric, and chili powder, then stir in the tomatoes and a little salt. Cook for 5 minutes, stirring occasionally.

3 Add the chicken and mix well, then pour in 1½ cups water. Bring to a simmer and cook gently for 15 minutes or until the chicken is cooked through. Serve sprinkled with the cilantro.

Bengali chicken curry

This recipe was given to me by a friend from Calcutta, an ancient and fascinating city. When I expressed my interest in the Bengalis' unique style of cooking, she gave me several recipes and this simple chicken dish was my favorite.

SERVES 4–6

1 lb skinless, boneless chicken thighs or breast
 halves, cubed
1/4 teaspoon ground turmeric
4 tablespoons vegetable oil
sea salt
3 tablespoons minced cilantro for garnish

FOR THE SPICE PASTE:

6 shallots, peeled and chopped
2 medium-hot green chili peppers, chopped
3 garlic cloves, peeled
1-inch piece fresh ginger, peeled and chopped
1 teaspoon ground mustard seeds
1/2 teaspoon ground turmeric

1 For the spice paste, place all the ingredients in a blender and process, adding a few tablespoons of water to make a smooth, thick paste.

2 Place the chicken in a non-metallic bowl. In another bowl, mix together the turmeric, a pinch of salt, and a tiny amount of water to make a smooth paste. Rub this mixture all over the chicken and set aside for 5–10 minutes or so.

3 Heat 2 tablespoons oil in a large frying pan or wok. Add the chicken and stir-fry over a medium heat for 10 minutes or until it is golden. Remove the pan from the heat and set aside.

4 Heat the remaining oil in another large saucepan. Add the spice paste and fry over a low heat for 2 minutes, then add the chicken and cook gently, stirring well, for 3–4 minutes. Pour in 1¼ cups water, cover the pan, and simmer gently over a medium heat for 15 minutes or until the chicken is cooked through. Sprinkle with the cilantro and serve hot.

duck curry

Duck is not a typical ingredient for most Indian people, but in Kerala, our beautiful backwater region, there are lots of ducks and several Christian dishes feature them. Goa and Mangalore, too, have some interesting duck curries.

SERVES 4–6

5 tablespoons vegetable oil

1/4 teaspoon fennel seeds

pinch of fenugreek seeds

2 large onions, peeled and sliced

2 medium-hot green chili peppers, chopped

1-inch piece fresh ginger, peeled and
    finely shredded

1 teaspoon ground turmeric

1/2 teaspoon hot chili powder

1 lb boneless duck breast, cubed

7 oz baby new potatoes, halved if large

1/3 cup wine or cider vinegar

13/4 cups coconut milk

few curry leaves, or to taste

sea salt

1   Heat the oil in a large saucepan. Add the fennel and fenugreek seeds, and stir-fry for 30 seconds. Add the onions, chilies, and ginger to the pan and fry over a medium heat for 5 minutes or until the onions are soft.

2   Sprinkle in the turmeric, chili powder, and a little salt. Mix well, then add the duck and potatoes. Stir-fry for 10 minutes or until lightly browned.

3   Pour in the vinegar, then stir in 1 cup of the coconut milk and 1 cup water. Lower the heat to medium-low, cover, and cook gently for 20 minutes, stirring occasionally.

4   When the duck is tender and the potatoes are well cooked, turn the heat right down and pour in the remaining coconut milk, stirring to combine. Gently mix in the curry leaves, then remove the pan from the heat and serve.

tikka

The marinated and grilled dishes known as tikka originated in India's northwest and can be traced farther back to Iran and its Persian cooking. In fact, ovens similar to the Indian tandoor can be found in many parts of central and near Asia. It is not possible to reproduce their intense, dry heat in the home kitchen; however, grilling and frying tikka foods still produces delicious results.

In recent years tikka dishes seem to have caught the British imagination, no doubt because it is a light and healthy way of enjoying spicy food. Chicken tikka seems to appear everywhere—even as a filling for sandwiches and wraps!

Chicken tikka masala is said to be the world's most popular Indian dish, yet it originated in English curry houses. This "marinated and grilled chicken in a creamy tomato sauce" appears in many guises. We have our own version and hope you like it! Each of the following tikka recipes serves 4.

▲ **lamb tikka with naan**
Rub the tikka marinade thickly and evenly over 1 lb cubed lamb. Marinate for 15–20 minutes, then thread onto 4 metal skewers. Heat 4 tbsp oil in a pan. Add the kebabs and cook, turning, for 10 minutes until brown and crisp on all sides. Meanwhile, sprinkle 4 naan breads with water and warm according to package directions. Serve the tikka with the naan, plus lime wedges, a tomato, cucumber and onion salad, and coconut or sweet mango chutney (page 31).

chicken or duck tikka

Rub the tikka marinade thickly and evenly over 1 lb cubed boneless chicken or duck breast halves, then marinate in a non-metallic dish for 15–20 minutes. Thread the meat onto 4 metal skewers or pre-soaked wooden skewers. Grill or broil for 5–10 minutes, turning frequently, until browned on all sides. You can also prepare salmon and thick white fish fillets, such as halibut, in this way.

▼ chicken tikka masala

Rub the tikka marinade thickly and evenly over 1 lb cubed boneless chicken breast halves, then let marinate for 15–20 minutes. Heat 4 tbsp vegetable oil in a pan and sauté 1 large chopped onion for 10 minutes until soft. Grind 4 garlic cloves and a 1-inch piece fresh ginger together to make a paste; add this to the pan and sauté for 2 minutes. Stir in ½ tsp ground turmeric, ½ tsp hot chili powder, and 1 tsp ground

▲ tikka marinade

Using a mortar and pestle, grind a 1-inch piece fresh ginger with 3 garlic cloves to make a smooth paste. Place in a bowl and add 1 cup plain yogurt, 1 tbsp lime juice, 1 tbsp chopped cilantro, ½ tsp hot chili powder, ¼ tsp ground turmeric, a large pinch of garam masala, and sea salt to taste. Whisk together until smooth, then use to marinate your chosen ingredients.

coriander. Add 1 tsp tomato paste, 1 cup chopped tomatoes, and 1 chopped green bell pepper; sauté for 2 minutes. Pour in 1½ cups water, bring to a boil, and cook, covered, for 20–25 minutes. Grill or broil the chicken until lightly charred. When the sauce is thick, lower the heat and pour in ¼ cup heavy cream. Add the grilled chicken and salt to taste. Heat through for a few minutes. Serve sprinkled with ¼ tsp garam masala and 2 tbsp chopped cilantro.

pork vindaloo

Vindaloo is a very traditional preparation from Goa, the famous tourist paradise. Pork dishes are not common elsewhere in India, but Goan cuisine has a strong Portuguese influence and the population is predominately Christian, so meat is used liberally. Locals love vindaloo's intense spicy flavor, which provides a good contrast to their milder, creamier coconut dishes. The traditional method is time-consuming and labor-intensive, so here is a modified version. Use beef, lamb, chicken, or shrimp, if you prefer.

SERVES 6–8

2 lb boneless pork, cubed
4 tablespoons vegetable oil
3 garlic cloves, peeled and chopped
2 onions, peeled and sliced
1 teaspoon ground turmeric
1/2 teaspoon hot chili powder
1 teaspoon tomato paste
3 tomatoes, chopped
3 tablespoons wine or cider vinegar
sea salt
cilantro leaves for garnish

FOR THE SPICE PASTE:

1 teaspoon cumin seeds
4 dried, hot red chili peppers
4 cardamom pods
4 whole cloves
1-inch piece cinnamon stick
10 black peppercorns
1-inch piece fresh ginger, peeled and
 chopped
4 garlic cloves, peeled
3 tablespoons wine or cider vinegar

1 To make the spice paste, put the cumin seeds, dried chilies, cardamom pods, cloves, cinnamon, and peppercorns in a small spice mill and grind to a fine powder. Transfer to a blender and add the ginger and the garlic. Add the vinegar and process to a smooth paste.

2 Place the pork in a large, non-metallic bowl, add the spice paste, and stir to coat well. Cover with plastic wrap and set aside to marinate in a cool place for 1½ hours.

3 Heat the oil in a large saucepan or heavy casserole. Add the garlic and sauté for 1 minute. Add the onions and cook gently for 10–15 minutes, stirring occasionally, until the onions are golden.

4 Add the turmeric, chili powder, tomato paste, chopped tomatoes, and 3 tablespoons vinegar. Mix well, then add the marinated pork and a little salt, and cook, stirring constantly, for 10 minutes.

5 Pour in 1 cup water and bring the mixture to a boil. Lower the heat, cover, and simmer gently for 30 minutes or until the meat is cooked through and the sauce is thick. Serve hot, with cilantro leaves scattered over the top.

lamb korma

Many people think of korma as a "safe" dish to order because of its mild taste, but in India it's not only mildness that's important—a creamy texture is essential too. In this case it's created with a paste made from cashew nuts. The same method can be used to make korma dishes with other meat or poultry. You may like to serve the korma with yogurt and a sprinkling of garam masala.

SERVES 4–6

1-inch piece fresh ginger, peeled and
  chopped
4 garlic cloves, peeled
3 tablespoons vegetable oil
1-inch piece cinnamon stick
3 whole cloves
2 bay leaves
3 cardamom pods, crushed
pinch of fennel seeds

2 onions, peeled and chopped
1 teaspoon ground coriander
1/4 teaspoon ground turmeric
1/2 teaspoon hot chili powder
2 teaspoons tomato paste
1 lb boneless lamb, cubed
pinch of ground black pepper
1/3 cup cashew nuts
1 tablespoon cilantro leaves
handful of toasted cashew nuts for garnish

1 Using a mortar and pestle, grind the ginger and garlic together to make a fine paste; set aside. Heat the oil in a saucepan, karahi, or wok. Add the cinnamon stick, cloves, bay leaves, cardamom, fennel seeds, and onions, and sauté for 5 minutes or until the onions are soft.

2 Add the ginger-garlic paste, then the ground coriander, turmeric, chili powder, and tomato paste. Mix well and cook over a low heat for 5 minutes, stirring occasionally. Stir in the lamb and black pepper, and pour in 2/3 cup water. Cover and simmer gently for 30 minutes or until the lamb is tender.

3 Meanwhile, using a mortar and pestle, grind the cashew nuts with a little water to make a smooth paste. When the lamb is cooked, add the cashew nut paste and stir well. Simmer for 3 minutes, then remove from the heat and serve, garnished with the cilantro leaves and toasted cashew nuts.

lamb with coconut slivers

I first came across this dish in a restaurant in New Delhi, where I started my catering career. It was the most popular item on the menu by a long way. People are fascinated by the spicy flavor of this dish, and the stronger the better—if you can handle it. Beef can be used in place of the lamb, if you prefer.

SERVES 4–6

1-inch piece fresh ginger, peeled and
  sliced
3 garlic cloves, peeled and chopped
1-inch piece cinnamon stick
2 bay leaves
3 whole cloves
20 curry leaves
5 tablespoons vegetable oil

2 onions, peeled and minced
1 tablespoon ground coriander
1/2 teaspoon ground turmeric
1/2 teaspoon hot chili powder
4-oz piece of coconut meat, shaved into slivers
1 lb boneless lamb, cubed
1/2 teaspoon mustard seeds
2 medium-hot green chili peppers, slit
  lengthwise

1 Using a small spice mill or mortar and pestle, grind the ginger, garlic, cinnamon stick, bay leaves, cloves, and 10 curry leaves together. Set aside.

2 Heat 3 tablespoons oil in a large saucepan, karahi, or wok. Add the onions and fry, stirring occasionally, for 5 minutes or until soft. Add the freshly ground spice mixture, the ground coriander, turmeric, chili powder, coconut slivers, and 1¾ cups water. Bring the mixture to a boil, then add the lamb. Lower the heat and simmer gently for 30 minutes or until the lamb is well cooked.

3 Heat the remaining oil in a separate small frying pan. Add the mustard seeds and, when they start to pop, add the remaining 10 curry leaves and the chilies. Stir-fry for 1 minute, then add the contents of the pan to the cooked meat and continue cooking, stirring frequently, for about 10 minutes or until the lamb mixture is very dry. Serve hot, with naan or other Indian bread.

lamb and potato curry

Chef Madhu introduced me to this style of lamb curry. While working at a famous restaurant in Delhi, he used to make the dish frequently for India's former chief minister. Madhu recommends a hot Malabar paratha (page 155) to accompany it, but any bread will do. Substitute beef for the lamb, if you prefer.

SERVES 4–6

5 tablespoons vegetable oil

1-inch piece fresh ginger, peeled and
   chopped

4 garlic cloves, peeled and chopped

2 medium-hot green chili peppers, chopped

15 curry leaves

2 onions, peeled and sliced

2 teaspoons ground coriander

½ teaspoon ground turmeric

½ teaspoon hot chili powder

3 tomatoes, sliced

1 lb boneless lamb, cubed

7 oz baby new potatoes, scrubbed

1 teaspoon mustard seeds

1 Heat 4 tablespoons oil in a saucepan. Add the ginger, garlic, chilies, and 5 curry leaves, and sauté for 3 minutes or until the ginger and garlic are golden brown. Add the onions and cook, stirring frequently, for 10 minutes until lightly browned.

2 Stir in the ground coriander, turmeric, and chili powder, and mix well, then add the tomatoes, lamb, and 1¾ cups water. Bring to a simmer and cook over a low heat for 15 minutes.

3 Stir in the new potatoes and continue simmering for 15 minutes or until the lamb is cooked and the potatoes are tender.

4 Meanwhile, heat the remaining 1 tablespoon oil in a small frying pan. Add the mustard seeds and, when they start to pop, add the remaining 10 curry leaves and stir well. Pour the contents of the frying pan over the lamb mixture and stir briefly, then remove the pan from the heat. Serve hot.

rogan josh

Almonds are a specialty of Kashmir and many parts of northern India. They are most commonly used in sweet dishes; however, rogan josh, a richly flavored lamb curry featuring ground almonds, is one exception. My friend Abdullah gave me this recipe. He is from Kashmir, where the dish is said to have originated. The combination of yogurt and almonds is unusual. I hope you like it.

SERVES 4

5 tablespoons vegetable oil

2 bay leaves

1 red onion, peeled and chopped

1 lb boneless lamb, cubed

1/3 cup ground almonds

sea salt

FOR THE SPICE PASTE:

2 cups plain yogurt

1-inch piece fresh ginger, peeled and
  chopped

2 teaspoons garam masala

1 teaspoon hot chili powder

1/2 teaspoon fennel seeds

large pinch of ground cardamom

1 To make the spice paste, place all the ingredients in a blender and process until smooth. Set aside.

2 Heat the oil in a large saucepan. Add the bay leaves and red onion, and sauté over a medium heat for 2 minutes.

3 Add the lamb and stir-fry for 5 minutes or until the meat is evenly browned. Slowly add the spice paste, stirring constantly to help the meat absorb the essence of the paste. Reduce the heat to low, cover, and cook gently for 30 minutes or until the lamb is tender.

4 Add the ground almonds and salt to taste. Serve hot with Malabar parathas (page 155).

stir-fried dry beef curry

In India, this spicy dish, known as *beef olathiathu,* is commonly served as a bar snack. It is very different from sauced curries, as the cooked beef cubes should be dry enough to pick up with the fingers. *Olathiathu* essentially means "stir-fried," and, although our method is very different from the Chinese style you may be familiar with, it is an important technique to give the meat the correct dry, yet succulent, texture. Feel free to make this dish hotter and spicier if you want to. Serve it with appams (pages 158–9), plus a moru curry (page 88–9), if desired.

SERVES 4-6

1 lb boneless beef round, cubed
1/2 teaspoon ground turmeric
1/2 teaspoon hot chili powder
3 tablespoons vegetable oil
5 garlic cloves, peeled and chopped
1 large onion, peeled and sliced
1 1/2 teaspoons ground coriander
1 teaspoon ground black pepper
1 teaspoon garam masala
20 curry leaves
sea salt

1 Place the beef, turmeric, and chili powder in a large saucepan or heavy casserole. Pour in 2 cups water and bring to a simmer, then cover and cook gently for 30 minutes or until the beef is tender. Add salt to taste, then remove the pan from the heat and set aside.

2 Shortly before the beef has finished simmering, heat the oil in a large frying pan, karahi, or wok. Add the garlic and sauté until it is brown, then add the onion and cook, stirring occasionally, for 10 minutes or until golden. Sprinkle in the ground coriander and sauté for 2 minutes.

3 Drain the excess liquid from the cooked beef mixture, then transfer the meat to the pan of spicy onions. Add the black pepper, garam masala, and curry leaves, and cook, stirring, over a medium heat for 10 minutes until the mixture is very dry. Serve hot.

7 breads and rice

pooris

These light breads are easy to make, look appetizing, and taste good. Poori masala—hot, puffy pooris served with freshly made potato masala—is one of the best breakfast dishes you will find in any part of India. It is a regular item in railway canteens and in home kitchens. Pooris are also excellent with dry chicken and lamb dishes.

MAKES 6

1¹/₂ cups all-purpose flour, plus extra for dusting
¹/₂ tablespoon vegetable oil
vegetable oil for deep-frying
sea salt

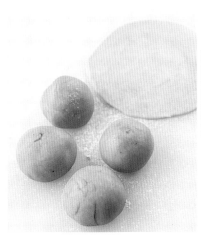

1   Place the flour in a large bowl with a generous pinch of salt. Gradually stir in the oil, then about ¹/₂ cup water or just enough to make a smooth dough. Cover and set aside for 10 minutes.

2   Knead the dough on a lightly floured work surface for 2–3 minutes. Divide the dough into six equal portions about the size of a golf ball. Roll out each ball as thinly as possible to make a neat round.

3   Heat the oil for deep-frying in a deep-fat fryer, wok, or large, heavy-based saucepan to 350°–375°F, or until a cube of bread browns in 30 seconds. At the same time, place a cast-iron griddle or a large, heavy-based frying pan over a high heat to heat thoroughly.

4   Working one at a time, toast the rounds of dough on the hot, un-oiled griddle for 30 seconds on each side. Then, using a spatula, transfer the poori to the hot oil and deep-fry for about 2 minutes, turning constantly to help it puff up. Remove from the pan and let drain on paper towels while you toast and deep-fry the remaining dough rounds. Serve as soon as they all are made.

chapattis

The majority of Indian people eat chapattis at most meals, serving them with curries or even simply a pickle. They are the most popular of all Indian breads, and you will find them on Indian restaurant menus all over the world. The ease with which they are made is a key advantage and they will complement most of the savory dishes in this book.

MAKES 8

3¹/₂ cups whole-wheat flour, plus extra
  for dusting
2 teaspoons vegetable oil
sea salt

1 Place the flour and a pinch of salt in a large bowl. Gradually stir in the oil, then mix in about 1 cup water to make a smooth dough.

2 Knead the dough on a lightly floured work surface for about 3 minutes, then divide the mixture into eight equal portions about the size of a golf ball. Working with one at a time, roll out the balls of dough as thinly as possible, turning them frequently to make an even round.

3 Heat a cast-iron griddle or large, heavy-based frying pan. When thoroughly hot, cook the chapattis, in batches as necessary: Place on the griddle and toast for 1–2 minutes on each side or until cooked and very lightly speckled brown, turning them frequently. Remove and keep warm while you cook the remaining chapattis. Serve as soon as they all are made.

Malabar parathas

This rich-tasting South Indian flat bread is invariably well received the first time anyone tastes it, and it is an essential order for regular customers at our restaurants. The dough is rolled and coiled to make a flaky bread that pulls apart temptingly in mouthwatering layers, yet it is made from a simple combination of whole-wheat flour and oil. Malabar paratha is an excellent accompaniment to Kerala's light vegetable curries.

MAKES 4

1 cup whole-wheat flour, plus extra
  for dusting
2 tablespoons vegetable oil, plus extra
  for oiling

1 Place the flour in a large bowl. Gradually stir in the vegetable oil and about ⅔ cup water or just enough to make a soft dough. Knead the dough on a work surface for 3–4 minutes, then return to the bowl, cover, and set aside to rest for 1 hour.

2 Divide the dough into four equal portions. Keeping the unused portions covered to prevent them from drying out, take one piece of dough and roll it into a ball, then dust lightly with flour.

3 On a clean work surface or board, roll out the dough to a round about 6 inches diameter. Brush the top lightly with a thin layer of vegetable oil. Roll up the dough to make a long, thin cigar shape, then carefully place one end of the dough in the middle of your palm and wind the rest around and around to make a coil.

4 Flatten the coiled dough with the palms of your hands and dust with flour. Return it to the work surface and carefully roll it out into a 5-inch round. Cover and set aside while you repeat the process with the remaining balls of dough.

5 Heat a cast-iron griddle over a medium-high heat for 8–10 minutes or until very hot. Place one or two parathas on it and sprinkle with a little oil. Cook, turning frequently, for 2–3 minutes on each side or until golden and cooked. Keep warm while you cook the rest, then serve warm.

adipoli parathas

Our special seafood-flavored bread is based on the popular Ceylonese tradition of flat, thin bread dough stuffed with a combination of spices and seafood masala. It has a wonderful rich flavor and crisp texture, and has been described as a complete meal in itself.

MAKES 8

2 cups whole-wheat flour, plus extra for dusting

4 tablespoons vegetable oil, plus extra for
   brushing

FOR THE FILLING:

1/2 cup vegetable oil

1/2 teaspoon mustard seeds

1-inch piece fresh ginger, peeled and grated

2 onions, peeled and minced

1 medium-hot green chili pepper, chopped

10 curry leaves

1/2 teaspoon ground turmeric

5 oz raw small shrimp, peeled

2 eggs, beaten

sea salt

1 To make the dough, place the flour in a large bowl. Gradually stir in the oil and about 2/3 cup water to make a soft, pliable dough. Knead on a work surface for 3–4 minutes, then return to the bowl, cover, and set aside for 1 hour.

2 To make the filling, heat the oil in a frying pan. Add the mustard seeds and, when they start to pop, add the ginger, onions, chili, and curry leaves. Cook over a medium-low heat for 5 minutes, stirring occasionally, until the onions are soft. Add the turmeric and a little salt, and sauté for 1 minute. Add the shrimp and cook for 7–10 minutes, stirring occasionally, until they have turned pink and are cooked. Remove the frying pan from the heat and set aside.

3 Divide the dough into eight equal portions. Place one piece in the palm of your hands and roll it into a smooth ball. Lightly dust with flour, then place it on a board and roll out as thinly as possible, to make a paper-thin round about 8 1/2 inches in diameter.

4 Heat a cast-iron griddle or large, heavy-based frying pan. Brush with oil and, when hot, add a round of dough. Stir the eggs into the shrimp mixture, then spread 3 tablespoons of this filling on top of the dough on the griddle. Cook over a medium heat for 5 minutes or until browned underneath.

5 Lower the heat, then carefully turn the paratha over with a spatula and cook for 5 minutes longer or until the shrimp mixture is well stuck to the paratha. Turn it over again and transfer the paratha to a board. Roll the paratha into a cylinder shape to enclose the shrimp mixture. Repeat with the remaining dough and filling. Cut each paratha into two or three pieces before serving.

appams

These soft, spongy pancakes, made from fermented white rice, are a typical dish of the Keralan Christian community. They are particularly popular at Easter, when they are served with lamb stew and other delicacies.

Appams have a naturally sweet flavor that is unique. They are also relatively easy to make. In the restaurants we like to be a little flamboyant, so we make them to order in front of customers, using a special curved pan called a chatti, which looks like a small cast-iron wok. However, they also look inviting cooked simply on a flat griddle or frying pan at home.

In Kerala, we tend to eat appams with mildly flavored stews, but they can also provide a good contrast to spicier dishes. Alternatively, you can serve them simply as a snack, with a good fresh chutney. However, my favorite way to eat appams is drizzled with a few tablespoons of coconut milk and sprinkled with a little sugar for breakfast.

▲ onion masala appams

Make the batter as for basic appams. Heat 2 tbsp oil in a pan, add ½ tsp mustard seeds, and, as they start to pop, add 10 curry leaves and 1 chopped red onion; cook for 5 minutes. Add 1 sliced medium-hot green chili pepper and cook for 2 minutes. Cook the appams as right, but after 2 minutes' cooking, gently spread 1 tbsp of the onion mixture on top. Carefully turn the appam over and cook for 3 minutes until the onion is golden and embedded in batter. Repeat to make 4–6 appams.

▼ basic appams

Wash 1½ cups basmati rice, then soak in fresh cold water to cover for 1 hour. Drain, reserving 1 cup water. Put the rice and reserved water in a blender and process to a batter. Add 1 cup freshly grated coconut and blend until fine; set aside. In a bowl, dissolve 1 tsp sugar in 5 tsp warm water, then add 1 tsp quick-rise active dry yeast; cover and set aside. Put ½ cup semolina in a pan with ½ cup water and cook for 15 minutes

egg appams

Make the batter as for basic appams. Heat an oiled griddle or nonstick frying pan. Add a ladleful of batter and spread thinly to make a large pancake. Cover and cook for 2 minutes, then remove the lid and crack an egg into the middle of the appam. Re-cover and cook for 2–3 minutes or until the base is golden and crisp, and the egg is lightly cooked. Transfer to a plate and serve. Repeat to make 4–6 egg appams.

or until thick. Transfer to a bowl. Add the rice batter and yeast mixture, stir well, and cover with a damp cloth. Set aside for 4 hours or until the batter is bubbly and doubled in volume. Gently stir in 1 tsp salt, taking care not to knock air out of the batter. Heat an oiled griddle or nonstick frying pan. Add a ladleful of batter and spread out thinly to make a large pancake. Cover and cook for 2 minutes on one side only, so the top remains moist; carefully remove from the pan. Repeat to make 4–6 appams.

▲ sweet appams

Make the batter as for basic appams. Just before cooking, mix 4 tbsp thin honey with 4 tbsp palm sugar, grated if necessary (or just use 6 tbsp honey). Heat an oiled griddle or nonstick frying pan. Add a ladleful of batter and spread out thinly to make a large pancake. Cover and cook for 2 minutes on one side only, so the top remains moist. Repeat to make 4–6 appams. Serve hot, drizzled with the honey mixture and sprinkled with freshly grated coconut, if desired.

vermicelli and rice

The first time I ate this rice and noodle dish in a Brahmin home, I thought it was delicious. Adding tempered spices gives a wonderful flavor and makes it more like a complete dish that could be eaten without curries alongside. Otherwise, it makes a good alternative to plain rice.

SERVES 4

3 tablespoons ghee
4 oz vermicelli
2 tablespoons vegetable oil
1/2 teaspoon mustard seeds
1 teaspoon dried urad dal
10 curry leaves
2 tablespoons cashew nuts

2 medium-hot green chili peppers, minced
1-inch piece fresh ginger, peeled and
  grated
1/2 cup freshly grated coconut
1/2 cup white rice, cooked
sea salt
2 tablespoons chopped cilantro, plus
  a few whole leaves, for garnish

1 Heat the ghee in a large frying pan over a medium heat. When hot, add the vermicelli and stir-fry for 5–6 minutes or until golden. Remove with a slotted spoon and set aside to drain on paper towels.

2 Heat the oil in another frying pan. Add the mustard seeds, urad dal, curry leaves, and cashew nuts, and fry for 1–2 minutes or until the nuts and urad dal turn brown. Add the chilies, ginger, and a little salt, then pour in 1 3/4 cups water and bring to a boil. Lower the heat, add the vermicelli, and simmer for 3–4 minutes until thoroughly blended with the spices.

3 Add the grated coconut and cooked rice. Carefully mix with the vermicelli and let warm through briefly. Transfer to a serving bowl, sprinkle with the cilantro, and serve.

boiled rice

Rice is a key part of any Indian meal. In Kerala, I was used to eating full-flavored, homegrown red rice, but in North India basmati rice is very popular because of its pure white color, clean flavor, and exotic fragrance. Basmati is now widely available everywhere and easy to cook.

SERVES 4

1 heaped cup white basmati or other
  long-grain white rice
sea salt

1 Wash the rice in plenty of cold water, then drain and place in a large, heavy-based saucepan. Add 3 cups fresh water and a little salt, and stir well. Place the saucepan over a high heat and bring to a boil. Lower the heat slightly and simmer for 20 minutes or until the rice is cooked. Drain thoroughly and serve hot.

vegetable rice

This is a variation of a colorful rice dish typically served with an array of dishes at special functions in India. Personally, I find it is delicious eaten on its own with a simple raita. The use of ghee gives it a special richness.

SERVES 4–6

2 medium-hot green chili peppers
1-inch piece fresh ginger, peeled and
   chopped
2 garlic cloves, peeled
2¹⁄₃ cups white basmati rice
4 tablespoons vegetable oil
¹⁄₂ teaspoon cumin seeds
1 cinnamon stick
5 cardamom pods
10 curry leaves

2 onions, peeled and minced
¹⁄₂ teaspoon ground turmeric
1 teaspoon hot chili powder
3 tomatoes, chopped
1 cup peeled and diced potato
1 cup cauliflower florets
¹⁄₂ cup green peas
2 tablespoons ghee
sea salt
2 tablespoons chopped cilantro for garnish

1   Using a small spice mill or mortar and pestle, grind the chilies, ginger, and garlic together to make a fine paste. Set aside. Wash the rice in plenty of cold water and set aside to drain thoroughly.

2   Heat the oil in a large saucepan. Add the cumin seeds, cinnamon, cardamom pods, and curry leaves, and sauté for 1 minute, then add the onions and cook over a medium heat for 5 minutes, stirring occasionally. Add the fresh chili paste and cook for 5 minutes or until the onions are golden. Add the turmeric, chili powder, tomatoes, and a little salt, and cook for 1 minute, stirring occasionally.

3   Add the rice, potato, cauliflower, peas, and ghee, and fry for 2 minutes. Pour in enough hot water to cover and give it all a stir. Bring to a boil, then lower the heat and simmer for 20 minutes or until the rice and vegetables are cooked. Transfer to a serving dish and sprinkle with the cilantro.

cashew and lemon rice

With its fresh citrus flavor and the fragrance of curry leaves, this lemon rice has become the most popular of the rice specialties served in our restaurants. In Brahmin homes lemon rice is considered a special occasion dish. Adding cashew nuts, which are prolific in Kerala, makes the dish taste much richer, and chana dal adds its own nutty flavor. In my view, all you need to make it a complete meal is a yogurt curry (see pages 88–9) and a delicious thoran (see pages 42–3). *Illustrated on previous page*

SERVES 4

1 heaped cup white long-grain or basmati rice
1/2 teaspoon ground turmeric
juice of 1/2 lemon
2 tablespoons vegetable oil
1 teaspoon mustard seeds
2 dried, hot red chili peppers
1 teaspoon dried chana dal or urad dal
3–5 curry leaves, plus extra for garnish
1/3 cup cashew nuts
sea salt

1   Wash the rice in plenty of cold water, then drain and place in a large, heavy-based saucepan. Add 3 cups water, the turmeric, and a little salt. Stir well and bring to a boil over a high heat. Lower the heat slightly and simmer for 20 minutes or until the rice is cooked. Drain thoroughly and return to the saucepan. Stir in the lemon juice and set aside in a warm place.

2   Heat the oil in a small frying pan. Add the mustard seeds and, when they start to pop, add the dried red chilies, chana dal, curry leaves, and cashew nuts. Stir-fry for 2–3 minutes or until the chana dal and cashew nuts are lightly browned, then pour the contents of the frying pan over the lemon rice.

3   Transfer the rice to a large serving dish, garnish with a few extra curry leaves, and serve.

Muslim-style rice with ghee

Biryani and similar richly flavored rice dishes are specialties of India's Muslim communities, but recipes vary widely around the subcontinent. In Kerala, the Malabar region is particularly known for its Islamic cooking, and this simple, yet delicious rice preparation is served with spicy meat dishes. I have found it excellent with mild curries, too. Ghee is normally associated with special rice preparations, but here its flavor is integral to the success of the dish.

SERVES 4–5

1¹/₂ cups basmati rice
6 tablespoons ghee
¹/₃ cup cashew nuts
1 tablespoon raisins
5 cardamom pods, lightly crushed
1 large onion, peeled and chopped
sea salt

1   Wash the basmati rice thoroughly in plenty of cold water, then drain and set aside in the strainer to drain thoroughly.

2   Heat the ghee in a large saucepan. Add the cashew nuts, raisins, and cardamom pods, and fry for 2–3 minutes until the cashews turn golden. Add the onion and cook, stirring frequently, for 5 minutes or until it is soft and lightly golden.

3   Stir in the drained rice and stir-fry for 5 minutes or until the rice grains are translucent. Add 4 cups water and a little salt. Bring to a boil, then lower the heat, cover the saucepan, and cook gently for 20 minutes or until the rice is tender and all the water has been absorbed. Serve hot.

8 desserts and drinks

Rasa fruit salad

We used to eat a lot of different fruits in our village, but fruit salad wasn't something I tried until I visited restaurants in the city. This one is a fantastic blend of various fruits and juices, and the perfect finish to a lovely meal.

SERVES 4–6

1 small pineapple
1 large wedge of watermelon
²⁄₃ cup seedless green grapes, halved
²⁄₃ cup seedless red grapes, halved
2 oranges
1 seedless guava or mango
¹⁄₂ cup mango juice
¹⁄₂ cup passion fruit juice
¹⁄₃ cup lime juice
¹⁄₃ cup shredded mint leaves

1 Cut away the skin from the pineapple and remove the "eyes," then quarter, core, and cut into chunks. Place the pineapple in a large bowl. Remove the skin and seeds from the watermelon, then cut into chunks. Add to the pineapple along with the grapes.

2 Peel the oranges, removing all white pith, then cut out the segments and add to the prepared fruit. Peel and chop the guava or mango and add to the bowl.

3 Pour the mango and passion fruit juices over the fruits and toss to mix. Add the lime juice and stir gently, then sprinkle with the mint. Serve in individual dishes, with a scoop of coconut or vanilla ice cream, if desired.

carrot pudding

In India, we make a number of desserts from carrots, including halwa, which is from the North. In South India, milky puddings called *payasam* are more popular. These are prepared in various ways, using different fruits, grains, and nuts. This pudding is a favorite at my sister's home.

SERVES 4

5 cups milk

pinch of powdered saffron

3 tablespoons ghee

2¼ cups grated carrots

¾ cup sugar

½ cup shelled pistachio nuts, skinned

3 tablespoons chopped blanched almonds

1 teaspoon ground cardamom

extra pistachio nuts and almonds for garnish
  (optional)

1 Pour 3 tablespoons of the milk into a small bowl, add the saffron, and set aside to infuse for 5–10 minutes until the milk is orange in color. Slowly bring the remaining milk to a boil in a large saucepan, then simmer over a medium heat for 10 minutes. Lower the heat and continue to simmer, stirring, for 20 minutes.

2 Meanwhile, heat the ghee in a frying pan. Add the grated carrots and gently fry for 5 minutes or until lightly golden.

3 Tip the carrots into a blender. Add the sugar and 4–5 tablespoons of the hot milk and process to a coarse paste. Add this to the simmering milk and stir well. Continue cooking over a low heat for 10 minutes.

4 Meanwhile, roughly grind the pistachios using a small spice mill or mortar and pestle. Add to the simmering carrot mixture with the chopped almonds, then mix in the saffron milk and cardamom. Simmer for a few more minutes, then remove from the heat. Serve hot or cold, topped with shredded almonds and pistachio nuts, if desired.

strawberry and banana pudding

This easy dessert was devised during one of my evening cooking classes. It was so successful it's now a regular item on our restaurant menus, too. You can use any ripe fruit, but I love the combination of banana and strawberries.
Illustrated on previous page

SERVES 4

5 tablespoons ghee
1/3 cup cashew nuts
1/3 cup raisins
3/4 cup palm sugar
1 3/4 cups coconut milk
pinch of ground cardamom
1 1/2 cups sliced strawberries
2 bananas, peeled and chopped

1 Heat 3 tablespoons ghee in a frying pan. Add the cashew nuts and fry for 2–3 minutes or until golden, adding the raisins after 1–2 minutes so that they plump up slightly. Remove the pan from the heat and set aside.

2 Put the palm sugar in a saucepan with 1 cup water and place over a low heat. Stir until the sugar dissolves, then increase the heat and simmer for 5 minutes. Add 2 tablespoons ghee and continue cooking for a further 5 minutes or until the sauce thickens.

3 Lower the heat, add the coconut milk, and simmer gently, stirring occasionally, for 10 minutes. Stir in the cardamom, then add the toasted cashew nuts and raisins. Remove the pan from the heat. Gently stir the strawberries and bananas into the sauce. Let cool before serving.

vermicelli pudding

This dessert is very popular in South India, especially among Tamil people. It is often presented as part of a thali meal in restaurants specializing in Tamil cuisine, which can be found all over India. It is also made at home for special occasions.

SERVES 4

7 oz vermicelli
6 tablespoons ghee
1/3 cup cashew nuts
1/3 cup raisins
5 cups milk
3/4 cup sugar
pinch of powdered saffron

1   Break up the vermicelli into short pieces, about 1¼ inches long, and set aside.

2   Heat the ghee in a large frying pan. Add the cashew nuts and gently fry for 2–3 minutes or until golden. Remove from the frying pan using a slotted spoon and set aside to drain on paper towels.

3   Add the raisins to the frying pan and fry, stirring, for 1 minute or until they are plump and toasted. Transfer them to the paper towels with a slotted spoon. Add the vermicelli to the frying pan and cook for 5 minutes or until it turns brown.

4   Bring the milk to a boil in a large, heavy-based saucepan over a medium heat. Simmer, stirring constantly, for 20 minutes or until the milk has reduced in volume by half. Lower the heat, then add the vermicelli and cook, stirring constantly, for 15 minutes.

5   Add the sugar, cashew nuts, raisins, and saffron. Simmer, stirring, for 5 minutes or until thoroughly blended. Serve the vermicelli pudding hot.

panchamritham

Panchamritham is a traditional dessert associated with the Palani temple in Tamil Nadu in South India. I once visited this temple with my father, who used to make regular pilgrimages there, and was amazed to see a street full of shops making panchamritham. There was no shortage of buyers. This dessert is simple to make and has a good clean taste of honey and fruits. If plantain is unobtainable, simply use two bananas rather than one.

SERVES 4

1 banana
1 plantain
1 mango
3 tablespoons ghee
1/3 cup halved and pitted fresh dates
1/3 cup raisins
1/4 cup sugar
3 tablespoons thin honey
pinch of ground cardamom

1 Peel and roughly chop the banana and plantain. Halve the mango, cut the flesh away from the pit, then cut into cubes and set aside.

2 Heat the ghee in a large frying pan. Add the banana, plantain, dates, raisins, and sugar, and fry gently for 5 minutes or until the mixture browns slightly and the fruits are well blended with the ghee.

3 Remove the pan from the heat. Add the honey, mango, and ground cardamom, and mix well. Set aside to cool, then chill until ready to serve.

mango halwa

Last year we held a mango festival and created many dishes using mangoes brought over from India, including this one. Halwa originates from the Muslim community and is normally time-consuming to make, but this is a simplified version. It has a delicious flavor and soft texture.

SERVES 4–6

4 tablespoons ghee

1/2 cup freshly grated coconut

1/3 cup semolina

1 lb well-drained canned mango

3/4 cup sugar, plus extra for sprinkling

1 large, fresh mango, peeled, pitted, diced, and well drained

1 teaspoon ground cardamom

chopped pistachio nuts for garnish

1 Heat 1 tablespoon ghee in a large frying pan. Add the coconut and fry for 3 minutes or until golden. Remove with a slotted spoon and set aside to drain on paper towels. Add the semolina to the frying pan and cook over a low heat for 5 minutes or until golden. Remove from the pan and set aside. Purée the canned mango pieces in a blender or food processor.

2 Put the sugar and 2½ cups water in a large, heavy-based saucepan. Heat slowly, stirring until the sugar dissolves, then increase the heat and bring to a boil. Add the mango purée and 2 tablespoons ghee. Turn the heat down to medium and cook for 35 minutes until well reduced, stirring frequently to prevent the mixture from sticking to the pan.

3 Add the remaining 1 tablespoon of ghee and cook for 15 minutes, stirring frequently, until the mixture is very thick. Sprinkle in the toasted semolina and cook for another 15 minutes or until the mixture is smooth and comes away easily from the sides of the pan.

4 Add the fresh mango, toasted coconut, and cardamom. Stir well, then pour the mixture into an oiled baking pan, about 10 by 8 inches. Let cool, then chill overnight until set. Cut into pieces and serve cold or at room temperature, sprinkled with pistachios and a little extra sugar.

kulfi

Kulfi, India's famously rich ice cream, is a regular feature on Indian restaurant menus in Europe and North America, but back home it is a cooling streetfood. Kulfi men on bicycles sell the ices to children and grownups alike. Everyone relishes the amazing taste, especially in summertime. The best fruit flavors change according to what is in season, but other varieties based on nuts and spices are made all year round.

Kulfi was first prepared for the grand Moguls, whose cuisine is Persian-influenced. In those days, clay pots were used as molds, but today lidded metal cones are more common. You can use any suitable freezerproof container, either individual molds about 6 oz capacity, or a large container—slice the ice cream to serve. Remember to soften kulfi at room temperature for 5 minutes before serving.

These recipes are based on my own style of kulfi-making. Each makes 8–10 servings.

▲ **mango kulfi**

Purée a drained 14-oz can mango pieces in a blender until smooth. Measure ⅔ cup mango purée and stir in a pinch of ground cardamom. Fold into the kulfi base with ⅔ cup heavy cream, lightly whipped. Freeze in a suitable container for 1 hour. Remove and whisk well, then freeze for another hour. Repeat the whisking and freezing twice more, then freeze, in individual molds, if desired, for 4–5 hours or overnight. Soften at room temperature before serving.

for the kulfi base

Bring 4 quarts (1 gallon) milk to a boil in a heavy-based pan. Lower the heat slightly and simmer for 45 minutes or until thickened and reduced by half. Cool slightly. In a bowl, mix 1 tbsp rice flour with 2 tbsp of the milk until smooth. Pour into the pan and cook for 15 minutes, stirring, until the milk has reduced to the consistency of a pourable sauce. Add 1 cup sugar and stir until dissolved. Let cool completely.

for a saffron kulfi base

Follow the method for the standard kulfi base, adding 1 tsp saffron threads to the reduced milk when you stir in the sugar.

almond kulfi

Fold ¼ cup ground almonds, ¼ cup sliced almonds, a few drops of almond extract, and ⅔ cup heavy cream, lightly whipped, into the cooled kulfi base. Freeze in a suitable container for 1 hour, then remove and whisk well. Return to the freezer for 1 hour. Repeat the whisking and freezing process twice more, then freeze, in individual molds, if desired, for 4–5 hours or overnight. Soften the kulfi at room temperature for 5 minutes before serving.

▲ pistachio kulfi

Add ⅓ cup crushed pistachio nuts and a few drops of rose water to the cooled kulfi base; mix well, then fold in ⅔ cup heavy cream, lightly whipped. Freeze in a suitable container for 1 hour, then remove and whisk thoroughly. Return to the freezer for 1 hour. Repeat the whisking and freezing process twice more, then freeze, in individual molds, if desired, for 4–5 hours or overnight. Soften the kulfi at room temperature for 5 minutes before serving.

Keralan lassi

In Kerala, this is the drink you will be offered on a hot afternoon. The fresh taste of spices with clean, thin, homemade yogurt is wonderfully refreshing and the best relief for hardworking farmers during their lunchbreak. Recently it has become the fashion to serve this drink in restaurants, where it has become known as Keralan lassi because of its spicy flavor.

SERVES 3–4

1¼ cups plain yogurt
1-inch piece fresh ginger, peeled and
  sliced
2–3 shallots, peeled and sliced
2 medium-hot green chili peppers, chopped
few curry leaves
pinch of cumin seeds
pinch of ground cumin
sea salt

1 Place the yogurt, ginger, shallots, chopped chilies, curry leaves, and a little salt in a blender. Add 1¼ cups water and process until smooth and thoroughly blended. Pour into a pitcher and chill until ready to serve.

2 Briefly toast the cumin seeds in a small frying pan over a medium heat until fragrant, then remove from the heat.

3 When ready to serve, place some crushed ice in each glass, pour in the lassi, and sprinkle with the ground cumin and toasted cumin seeds.

banana lassi

This is one of my favorite drinks—it was my regular order at the refreshment kiosk during my school years. The thought of flavorful bananas blended with cold yogurt, our local sugar, and a touch of cardamom still makes my mouth water.

SERVES 2–4

1 cup plain yogurt
1^1/2 cups cubed bananas
^{1}/2 cup milk
4 teaspoons sugar
^{1}/2 teaspoon ground cardamom
1 tablespoon pistachio nuts, crushed

1   Place the yogurt, bananas, milk, and sugar in a blender and blend until very smooth. Stir in the ground cardamom.

2   Place some crushed ice in a pitcher or individual glasses and pour the lassi over. Sprinkle with the crushed pistachio nuts and serve.

almond milk shake

I am very partial to this Indian-style milk shake. It's a lovely combination of flavors and is very tasty served chilled.

SERVES 4

2 tablespoons blanched almonds
2 tablespoons pistachio nuts
2 cups milk
2 tablespoons brown sugar
^{1}/2 teaspoon ground cardamom

1   Place the almonds and pistachio nuts in a blender, add ^{1}/2 cup water, and work to a coarse paste. Add the milk and brown sugar, and process for 2 minutes or until smooth and well blended.

2   Divide the milk shake among 4 serving glasses. Add some crushed ice, then sprinkle with ground cardamom and serve immediately.

tangy carrot juice

I have fond memories of New Delhi juice bars, which offer the best selection of juices I have ever seen. People in North India consume a lot of different fresh juices and I am fascinated by their clever use of spices to make the drinks more interesting. My favorite additions to carrot juice are fresh mint and ginger.

SERVES 4

1 lb carrots, peeled
1-inch piece fresh ginger, peeled and
  chopped
1 tablespoon mint leaves
2 tablespoons lime juice
sea salt

1 Cut the carrots into chunks, then push them through a juice extractor with the chopped ginger and mint leaves. Transfer the carrot juice to a pitcher and add sea salt to taste and the lime juice. Chill well before serving.

cardamom tea

Spiced milky tea is hugely popular in India, and can be made with either complex spice blends or simple ones. This version is made using green cardamom pods, which have a sweet lemony flavor, plus fresh ginger. For authenticity, use Assam tea, which is a full-bodied style from northeast India.

SERVES 4

1 cup + 2 tablespoons milk
2 tablespoons Assam tea leaves
1-inch piece fresh ginger, peeled and
  grated
5 green cardamom pods
sugar to taste

1 Pour the milk into a small saucepan, add 1 cup water, and bring to a boil. Lower the heat slightly and add the tea leaves, ginger, cardamom, and sugar to taste. Simmer gently for 5 minutes, stirring occasionally to ensure that the ingredients are well mixed.

2 Remove the pan from the heat and discard the cardamom pods. Pour the cardamom tea into cups and serve immediately.

watermelon and lime juice

When summer temperatures are high, there is nothing better than this superb, refreshing juice. I hope you like it as much as I do.

SERVES 4

½ small watermelon
2 tablespoons lime juice
1–2 tablespoons sugar, or to taste (optional)
4 thin lime slices

1 Cut away the rind from the watermelon and remove the seeds with a teaspoon. Cut the flesh into manageable pieces. Push the watermelon flesh through a juice extractor. Alternatively, you can purée the watermelon in a blender, then strain the juice.

2 Transfer the watermelon juice to a pitcher and add the lime juice. Taste and sweeten with a little sugar, if required, mixing well. Chill the juice until ready to serve.

3 To serve, pour the chilled watermelon juice into 4 serving glasses. Add some crushed ice and a lime slice to each glass.

index